DAISY ASHFORD
Her Life

DAISY ASHFORD
Her Life
by R. M. Malcomson

CHATTO & WINDUS

THE HOGARTH PRESS

LONDON

Published in 1984 by
Chatto & Windus · The Hogarth Press
40 William IV Street
London WC2N 4DF

British Library Cataloguing in Publication Data

Malcomson, R. M.
Daisy Ashford.
1. Ashford, Daisy—Biography
2. Authors, English—20th century—Biography
I. Title
823'.912   PR6001.S44Z/

ISBN 0 7011 2787 2

Photoset by Rowland Phototypesetting Ltd
Bury St Edmunds, Suffolk
Printed in Great Britain by
St Edmundsbury Press
Bury St Edmunds
Suffolk

Title page
Daisy drawn by her sister Vera

CONTENTS

ACKNOWLEDGEMENTS

In the research necessary for this book I have been lucky enough to have in my possession many letters and souvenirs of the nineteenth century, preserved by my mother, Vera Lowther, and have based my story very largely on them, and on a memoir by my mother and her letters.

I am particularly indebted to my cousin, Margaret Steel, Daisy's elder daughter, who has lent photographs, read the typescript at its different stages and allowed me to quote from Daisy's letters and writings. I would also like to thank my cousins, Clare Rose, Terence O'Connor, Pixie Tyas and Helen Alford for lending material and for remembering so many stories; Sister Mary Brigid of The Priory, Mrs Walker-Munro, Sir William Barber, The National Coal Board (now occupying Eastwood Hall), and the County Library Headquarters at Southdown House, Lewes who allowed me to photograph the house; also Mrs Dewhurst (the owner of Byam Cottage), Mrs Marley-Fletcher, Mr Gordon, Mr David Chadwick for his research into the Walker family, and the many other people who have helped me.

But my chief thanks are due to the three Ashford sisters for their vivid and amusing memories of the people and events of long ago – those memories of memories on which I have been able to draw.

Arundel, Sussex, February 1984

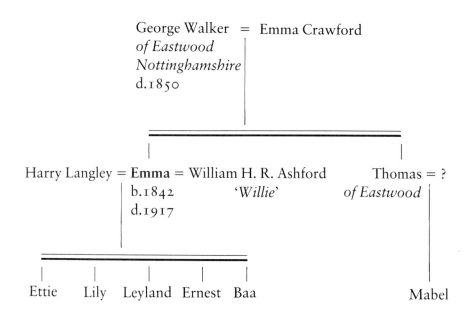

George Walker = Emma Crawford
of Eastwood
Nottinghamshire
d.1850

Harry Langley = **Emma** = William H. R. Ashford   Thomas = ?
            b.1842   '*Willie*'   *of Eastwood*
            d.1917

Ettie   Lily   Leyland Ernest Baa   Mabel

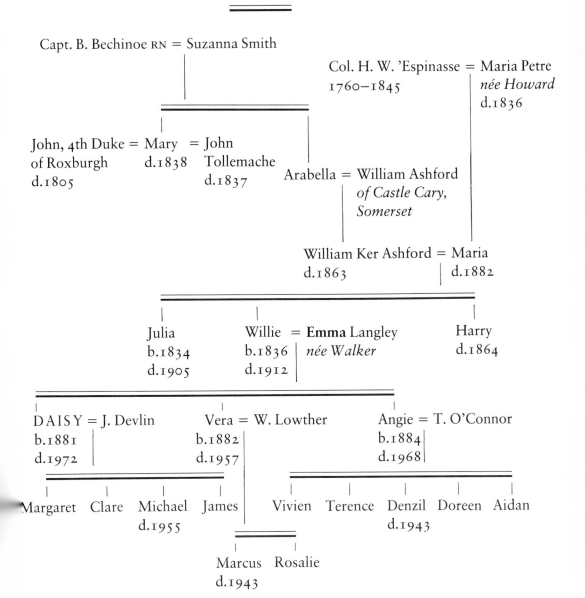

Capt. B. Bechinoe RN = Suzanna Smith

Col. H. W. 'Espinasse = Maria Petre
1760–1845   *née Howard*
         d.1836

John, 4th Duke = Mary   = John
of Roxburgh   d.1838   Tollemache
d.1805   d.1837

Arabella = William Ashford
         of Castle Cary,
         Somerset

William Ker Ashford = Maria
d.1863   d.1882

Julia   Willie   = **Emma** Langley   Harry
b.1834   b.1836 | *née Walker*   d.1864
d.1905   d.1912

DAISY = J. Devlin   Vera = W. Lowther   Angie = T. O'Connor
b.1881   b.1882   b.1884
d.1972   d.1957   d.1968

Margaret   Clare   Michael   James   Vivien   Terence   Denzil   Doreen   Aidan
               d.1955   d.1943

Marcus   Rosalie
d.1943

INTRODUCTION

Daisy Ashford was born on 7th April 1881, at Elm Lodge in Petersham, Surrey, the home of her paternal grandmother, and of her aunt, Julia Ashford, whose doting attention contributed largely to that faintly smug expression evident in early photographs. She was the eldest of the three Ashford sisters, born to middle-aged parents, and into a family where late marriages were common. Her father was born in the reign of William IV and well remembered his grandfather, who was born in 1760. The oral tradition of such extended generations reaches much further back than is usual in most families, and the children of old parents may often feel themselves to be not quite like their contemporaries from having learned their manners and way of speech from people older not by one, but by two generations. Neither was Daisy's mother a typical Victorian: her eccentricity and bluntness would have been less noticeable in the eighteenth century.

In reading the letters that passed between various members of the Ashford family in the nineteenth century it is hard to discover a subject in which they were not interested (always excepting science). Well educated and well read, they were also very musical, keen concert and opera goers; several of them drew and painted well and wrote knowledgeably on art. The theatre, politics and world affairs were commented on; they broke into verse with ease and wrote thoughtful appraisals of the books they read. Apt quotations sprang to their lips or were dashed off in their letters.

In order to understand the character and the talent of Daisy Ashford one needs to know something more about the family and antecedents of a girl who began writing at the age of four and produced what J. M. Barrie called her masterpiece when she was nine.

PART I

The Ashford Family

———

The Ashfords were an old west country family; there is mention of a Florence Ashford marrying into the Fraunceis family of Combe Florey in Somerset in the fifteenth century and in 1620 an Arthur Ashford is recorded as living in Wonwell in Devon. The family settled later in both Castle Carey and Shepton Mallet, country gentlemen with a little land, and whose sons became local solicitors or clergymen. And they might have enjoyed many more comfortably provincial years had not a William Ashford at the end of the eighteenth century married an Arabella Bechinoe. One of Arabella's sisters, Mary, had married a man many years her senior who was distantly related to the 3rd Duke of Roxburgh. An astonishing series of deaths of the heirs male resulted, in 1804, in her husband becoming the 4th duke, a dignity which he enjoyed for only one year before dying and leaving the duchess a childless widow and immensely rich. Being also very affectionate and kind-hearted she was able to give generous allowances to her three sisters, and she stood godmother to Arabella's son, William (Daisy's grandfather), who was born in the year of her widowhood, and who was given the second name of Ker in her honour. It was understood that he was to be her heir, and Arabella and her family moved, about this time, to Twickenham. William became a great favourite with his aunt, and his future seemed well assured until the duchess married again, a wedding marred by the arrest for debt of the bridegroom at the church door. The bride, of course, was obliged to pay up and the very natural feelings of the Ashfords can be imagined as the future prosperity of their son seemed to hang in the balance. But the duchess, for so she continued to call herself, failed to bear any children and the allowances continued to flow.

William was sent to Harrow and on to Trinity College, Cambridge, returning to live at home in 1828. He was then twenty-three, a slight young man with the brown hair and grey eyes of his family, regular features and broad forehead. He was also sociable, kind-hearted and virtuous, and had laid the foundations of the two main interests of his life, book collecting and drawing. He became an excellent artist, filling pocket sketch-books with views of the sea shore, old cottages, fishing boats and the Thames at Twickenham, as well as painting portraits of his family. He was admirably fitted for the life of leisure that had been mapped out for him.

Aunt Roxburgh loomed large in his life, descending from time to time into England from her home at Broxmouth, on the Scottish borders, to visit her sisters and to stay in her London house. She used also to stay at Ham House, across the river from Twickenham, for the owner, Lady Dysart, who had been born in the year of Culloden, was the mother of her second husband.

In 1832 William married Maria 'Espinasse, the daughter of an army officer of Huguenot descent who had, ironically, married one of the Howards of Corby in Cumberland, a family who had remained staunch-ly Catholic throughout penal times. It was her second marriage and they were both middle-aged when Maria was born. It was a period when the daughters of a mixed marriage were brought up in the religion of their mother and the sons of their father, so the flight from France of Colonel 'Espinasse's ancestor was nullified, and the strong Catholic strain was brought into the Ashford family.

It is important to understand the religious atmosphere which prevailed in the first part of the nineteenth century. From the sixteenth century Catholics had lived under heavy religious, legal and social restrictions: fines for non-attendance at the services of the Church of England, imprisonment for harbouring priests and death in its most barbarous forms. They had banded together in groups, very often round a Catholic landowner, so that there were enclaves of the old religion dotted about the country. Their numbers had dwindled to 50,000 at one time. They felt like a besieged garrison, outcasts in their own country.

Towards the end of the eighteenth century, however, means were taken to remedy the many injustices suffered, and after the set-back of the Gordon Riots, feeling gradually changed until, in 1829, the Catholic

Mary, Duchess of Roxburgh. *c.* 1810

From William Ashford's sketchbook. Two of many studies of the complexities of sailing and the Sussex coast. *c.* 1840

Ham House, home of the Tollemache family, who owned much of Ham and Petersham including Elm Lodge. *Below*: Ham meadows, *c*. 1840, by William Ashford

Emancipation Act was passed, and Catholics, so to speak, crept out of the woodwork that they had entered in Elizabeth's reign; they were, on the whole, cautious, in-bred, steadfast, often eccentric, and with a piety that was medieval in its intensity. Many of their religious practices had remained unchanged since the sixteenth century, so that English Catholics were often embarrassing strangers to the papacy for whom their ancestors had suffered. Shortly after the Emancipation Act came the surge of the Oxford Movement, when both Protestants and Catholics found themselves stirred in an invigorating wind of religious fervour. Catholic schools and churches were built, many to cater for the Irish who were coming over in their thousands, and every Catholic felt it a duty to help in all the organising, building and charitable work that had become necessary.

This was the climate into which William and Maria were married and their children brought up. Their first child was Julia, born in 1834, followed by Willie (Daisy's father) in 1836. Two more boys followed, one of whom died in infancy and the other as a young man. The boys were baptised in the Church of England and Julia in the Catholic Church. And such was the toleration and affection among them that this does not seem to have caused any rancour.

According to family tradition Maria was a woman of strong character and strong feelings. She had a great talent for friendship and was a favourite sister and aunt, always ready to help or lend a sympathetic ear. She wrote and spoke French and Italian, and her handwriting, sloping and even, and looking as though executed with a sharpened pin, adorns the flyleaves of many volumes in those languages. She was sufficiently musical to volunteer, after her marriage, to teach a friend's daughter the piano, and she was, like her mother, a devout Catholic. This piety she passed on to Julia. Together they went to Mass at nearby Isleworth, and as Julia grew up she began to take part in the practices of the church that have now largely disappeared: the long fasts of Lent and Advent, days of abstinence from meat, Ember Days, the long and beautiful liturgy of Holy Week, and procession of the Blessed Sacrament at Corpus Christi. All the great Latin hymns and the Gregorian chants she grew to love.

Julia was the perfect elder sister, the confidante and often the accom-

Left: Maria 'Espinasse aged 18. 1820

Below: Julia and Willie, miniatures by William Ashford, 1839

plice of her brothers, but from the first the bond between her and Willie was the strongest. Both had a love of books and music, poetry and history, scenery and travelling. Letters flowed between them commenting on the latest books, the singers of the day, the choirs and concerts they had heard, as well as political and military events. But above all, in both brother and sister there was a well of religious feeling and thought that developed during their lives, growing from a simple piety to a deep spirituality. This was a great part of the bond between them and it was because his children recognized this strength in Willie that they turned to him and not to their mother for help or advice.

In 1838 occurred the event for which, in a sense, William had been waiting all his life. The Duchess of Roxburgh died and was buried in a vault purchased the previous year from the General Cemetery Company at Kensal Green, and in which her second husband had already been laid. At a meeting of her near relations it was disclosed that she had made no will and that her lavish style of living and, no doubt, her late husband's propensity to run up debts, had drained away most of her money. At the end of six years of selling her many possessions and trying to collect old rents there was a Final Settlement which satisfied no one. William, after the first disappointment, accepted in a philosophical spirit that he would never be a rich man, although he was still comfortably enough off to be able to send both his sons to Eton. Julia, naturally, stayed at home to be educated by a governess.

In 1852 the family settled in Petersham, then a delightful village, though with more than the normal village's share of large, elegant houses. They rented Elm Lodge, a pleasant early Georgian house, part of the Ham estate, with large gardens, stables, cowshed, orchard and fields, seven acres in all, in which they kept the two cows that supplied the household with milk. Sixteen years earlier Dickens had rented it and had written much of *Nicholas Nickleby* there. William and Maria Ashford were to spend the rest of their lives here, near their old friends across the river in Twickenham and close to Richmond with its new Catholic church and the railway station.

By the age of nineteen Julia had far outstripped her mother in learning and was quite as good a Latin scholar as Willie. She spoke and wrote German, French and Italian and could uphold her opinion in argument. She wrote verses with ease and both played and sang extremely well. Far from being alarming, however, in her many accomplishments, she had a lively sense of humour and was quite without pride. In looks, though her eyes slanted attractively, she was never a beauty or a woman of fashion; it was her sweetness of disposition and her beautiful manners that endeared her to people. She was launched into Catholic society on a round of visits to cousins in the north where she thoroughly enjoyed herself at balls and picnics, playing billiards and arguing a more charitable attitude towards the Church of England than that shown by some of her relatives. Later on she would often go to hear the singing or the sermons in Protestant churches, an act which most Catholics of her day would have found embarrassingly close to the forbidden 'taking part in the services and prayers of a false religion' of the catechism.

At the age of twenty-one she became engaged to an army officer, but he died of fever in the Crimea and there is no mention of his name in her surviving papers, only a note at the end of her Bible, 'Nov. 28th, 1855. *Requiescat in pace.* I shall go to him but he shall not return to me.' And many years later she wrote:

> I sometimes when the day is o'er,
> Call up the vanished past again,
> And live it over yet once more
> And say, 'But few short years remain.'
> And trust when I have striven my best,
> And those around me, smiling, say,
> 'See how Time makes all grief decay,'
> To lie down thankfully to rest
> And meet thee in eternal day.
>
> Eternal form shall still divide
> The eternal soul from all beside
> And I shall know him when we meet.

Julia in the 1860s

Elm Lodge, Petersham in the 1850s.
Left to right: Gardener, Harry, Maria,
Willie, William and Julia

Willie, while Julia was entering society, was finishing his education. He had become a good Latin and Greek scholar, a keen cricketer and oarsman and a heroic walker, often covering thirty miles in a day. He considered ten miles the very mininum for daily exercise. He resembled his father in looks and in character, but while his father was an artist, Willie had a passion for music, especially choral music. Many pro- grammes survive of Handel Festivals he attended, concerts in which he sang and the musical evenings so beloved of the Victorians. There still exist bound scores of Handel, Mozart, Beethoven and the nineteenth- century composers, that belonged to him.

When he was a young man his mother complained that he was not lively enough in company, while his younger brother, Harry, appears to have been very sociable from an early age, and with an eye for the girls. But Willie was reserved, and no hint of any passing fancy is given in any of Julia's letters, while she discussed at length Harry's latest love, usually some stage beauty whom he admired from afar. After his early diffidence, however, Willie was much in demand at parties because of his agreeable manners and fine voice. He entered the Ordnance Department at the War Office, walking daily from Petersham to London and back, sometimes deviating from his route to call on friends. And he joined the Volunteers, a subject of some amusement to Harry, who became a cadet at the Royal Military College at Woolwich.

Letters, mostly Julia's, indicate a cheerful, loving family atmosphere. A bundle of Harry's letters show how well he and Willie got on, and how frequently Willie used to visit his brother wherever he was stationed. A few letters from his father to Willie have survived, humorous and affectionate, and referring to walks the two had taken and the pleasure of a long, lazy day in the garden drinking beer and smoking.

In 1863, at the early age of fifty-eight, William Ashford died suddenly and to Willie now fell family duties and the local charitable activities that his father had performed, and Julia had to sacrifice much of her own time to be with her mother. And while they were still in mourning for William another blow fell. A telegram arrived from Harry's regiment in Malta informing them of his death. In the space of a few months the whole character of the family had changed, and Willie and Julia were inevitably drawn closer.

For the next sixteen years they lived tranquilly with their mother at Elm Lodge, during which time there were only two events of any importance. The first was Willie's resignation from the War Office. He was then only thirty-five and what prompted this apparently foolhardy decision remains a mystery. He evidently had no other post in mind, although from letters written at the time it appears that he applied for several over the next few years. That he needed some sort of paid employment to supplement his income is shown by a letter from Julia in 1872, 'What think you of the enclosed advert.? It might be worth thinking about.' The advertisement pinned to the top of her letter was for the post of vestry clerk to the parishes of St Margaret and St John the Evangelist at Westminster where 'an experienced and competent person' was required at a salary of £300 a year.

The second event was his reception into the Catholic Church, a step that he had contemplated for years, and no doubt his mother and sister had been expecting as long. He immediately became active in local Catholic affairs, and went daily to Mass and to annual retreats at the various centres round England.

Willie was approaching middle age now and Maria was over seventy, so it was natural that Julia should look to the future when she and Willie would be on their own, the bachelor and the spinster who agreed so well and were so devoted to each other. They should retire, she decided, to a small house, perhaps by the sea, and live out their days happily busy together. What Willie felt about these plans we do not know, but in 1880, when he was forty-four, something happened that was to change their lives. Canon Bagshawe, their parish priest, introduced him to the widow with five young children who was to become his wife.

TRIENNIAL

HANDEL FESTIVAL,

CRYSTAL PALACE, 1865.

On FRIDAY, JUNE 30TH,

WI]

HAND

ISRAEL

Recit. .. Mr. CUMM
Solo and { M
Chor

PROGRAMME

OF THE

AMATEUR CONCERT

AT THE

LARGE ROOM OF THE NATIONAL SC

ETON STREET, RICHMOND.

On TUESDAY EVENING, JUNE 9,

COUNT EMILE WROBLESKI,

Pianist to the Emperor of Brazil, has kindly consente

MISS EMMA JENKINS,

AND

MR. WADSWORTI

Doors open at 7.15.   *Carriages at 10 15*

Richmond Musical Society.

ESTABLISHED 1858.

President:

C. JASPER SELWYN, Esq. M.P.

Vice-Presidents:

PETER FITZGERALD, Esq.	BRANDRAM PEELE, Esq.
H. C. LACY, Esq.	R. SMITH, Esq.
G. F. WHITELEY, Esq.	

THE MEMBERS OF THE ABOVE SOCIETY ARE HEREBY INFORMED
THAT

THE FIRST SOIRÉE OF THE SEASON

WILL TAKE PLACE IN THE

NATIONAL SCHOOL ROOM, ETON STREET,

On Monday Evening, November 7th, 1859,

TO COMMENCE AT EIGHT O'CLOCK PRECISELY.

PROGRAMME FOR THE FIRST SOIRÉE.

MILITARY SYMPHONY (No. 12)—Adagio & Allegro,	*Haydn.*
PART SONG—" See the Chariot,"	*Horsley.*
MILITARY SYMPHONY—Allegretto	*Haydn.*
CHORUS—" Sancta Maria," (Dinorah)	*Meyerbeer.*
OVERTURE—Semiramide	*Rossini.*
SONG—" The King and the Kaisir,"	*F. Mori.*
PART SONG—" My Love is like the Red Rose," ..	*Knyvett.*
OVERTURE—Masaniello	*Auber.*

Ladies and Gentlemen wishing to become Members, can obtain every
information at Mr. ETHERINGTON's, or Mr. ABBOTT's, Music Sellers, as by
the Rules now established, no one is admissible to the Concerts or Soirées,
unless a Member, or holding a Member's Ticket.

The first CONCERT of the Society will take place about the end of November,
of which due notice will be given.

T. F. DARNILL, PRINTER, COLUMBIAN OFFICE, KING STREET, RICHMOND.

Page 26: Some concert programmes. Music was an essential part of life in the family

Page 27: W. H. R. Ashford – 'Willie' – as a young man

Julia aged about 20

Willie as a Volunteer in the 1850s, when he was already working at the War Office

William Ashford in middle age

PART II

The Walker Family

For the lives of Daisy's maternal grandparents, George and Emma Walker, the chief sources of information are family tradition and official records; no letters, pressed flowers, concert programmes or mementoes, such as the Ashfords preserved so carefully, have survived. Mrs Walker's name appears, it is true, on the flyleaves of half a dozen books, among them Tupper's *Proverbial Philosophy*, Moore's *Irish Melodies* and a volume entitled *Is it possible to make the best of both worlds?* – her taste in reading being one of the few clues to her character.

The Walkers were a prolific Nottinghamshire family, hard-working and ambitious: Coal Masters and Iron Masters, who were mining in the reign of Queen Anne. From that time they steadily increased their mining activities and became canal and railway builders (George Walker was a founder of the Midland Counties Railway, which later became the familiar LMS Railway). They owned extensive farming land, and speculated successfully in town property and the stock market. By the time George married he was a rich man who lived for and near his work, in an elegant white Regency house on the outskirts of Eastwood near Nottingham. There were stables and coach house on a grand scale, and a large walled garden whose cavity walls contained a system of hot water pipes to protect from the frost the peach trees that spread their branches over the bricks. And there were also an orchid house and vinery.

In selecting his wife George showed a glaring lack of common sense, but she was very attractive, and their incompatibility did not emerge until after their marriage in 1841. Tough and ambitious himself, he was inclined to regard the new Mrs Walker as a meek and helpless woman whom he could direct and mould when the cares of his work permitted. But she was not to be moulded. Extravagant and well-connected, she spent her allowance freely, and her time in visiting her sisters, going to balls and entertaining at Eastwood. A memorable sentence uttered by him on seeing her at breakfast in a low-cut gown has been handed down to his descendants. 'I see, my dear, that you have appeared in a state of semi-nudity which, during the course of the day will, no doubt, become total.'

A year after their marriage Emma Georgina (Daisy's mother) was born, and three years later, in 1845, her brother, Tom. They both took after their mother in character, but fortunately George died before he could realise this, leaving a will whose complexity was only equalled by his obvious concern that his children should not be married for their money as he had been. He gave instructions about hypothetical descendants to the second and third generations. Daughters, real and imaginary, were hedged about with stipulations as to their choice of husbands, who had to be vetted by three trustees. He even set time limits on the birth of grandchildren who would benefit from his estate. He died under the impression that he had catered for every eventuality, and that the carefree, happy blood of his wife would be diluted by the prudent marriages of her descendants.

George's widow had every inducement to remain single – the use of Eastwood Hall during Tom's minority and a handsome allowance which would be withheld if she remarried. The children were free of their father's disapproving presence and could give full rein to their natural high spirits. Tom was sent to Eton and Emma was educated at home, and grew up to be strong and independent, with a love of riding and with her mother's cheerful disregard for economy. Her appearance was striking. She had thick, dark hair, very long and fine, and dark brown eyes, and although she was never beautiful like her mother, she was extremely attractive to men and retained all her life an irresistible vitality and humour that made her excellent company. When she was eighteen she was offered the choice of a season in London or a season of hunting, and she unhesitatingly chose hunting. Her brother, on leaving Eton, showed an equal enthusiasm for cricket and a ground was laid out in the park, and a team formed, called The Jolly Dogs. Emma's function during their matches was scorer or 'notcher' – she cut notches in a stick to mark the runs.

Emma's aunt, Lady Bolton, who lived in Yorkshire, was very fond of her niece and, being of a match-making turn, introduced Emma to a most eligible peer, and to her satisfaction they became engaged. Emma was now twenty-one.

Unfortunately, before the marriage could take place, another man entered her life, Harry Langley, a dashingly good-looking cornet in the 11th Hussars, and Emma fell headlong in love with him. Consulting no one, they eloped and were married in Nottingham, and then, in considerable disgrace with her family and fiancé, they moved to Dublin to join Harry's regiment.

Emma, accustomed to a comfortable standard of living, received every encouragement from Harry, for he himself was a big spender, although lacking in means. They took a house in a fashionable part of Dublin, the drawing-room of which Emma redecorated with pale green pleated silk wall hangings. Inevitably her dress allowance (all that she could get from the trustees) and Harry's pay were not enough to meet the bills that poured in, so they appealed to Harry's father to help them out of their difficulties. He arrived in Dublin and was appalled at their extravagance. Taking Harry to one side, he was about to unburden himself, when Harry began telling him an amusing story he had just heard, and before long the older Mr Langley was laughing heartily. 'Now, Father, you see you're laughing,' his son pointed out in some relief. 'If I was laughing,' replied Mr Langley with dignity, 'it was with disgust.'

According to George Walker's will, which even the lawyers found difficult to understand, a large portion of his estate would come to Emma if she produced a son within a specified period, and in 1864 the Langleys moved back to England, to Lady Bolton (who had evidently forgiven her), where her first child was to be born. Tom, accompanied by his solicitor, travelled north to see fair play, and the anxiety of the two young men can be imagined as they waited together in an adjoining room for the birth. It was a girl.

They returned to Ireland, and Harry, after only one year in the army, retired. He continued, good-looking and popular as ever, to hunt, shoot and fish, and enjoy the devastation his charm caused among the ladies.

The imminent birth of another child sent them hurrying back to Lady

Bolton. Tom and his lawyer arrived from Eastwood once more, for Emma was to have her second and last chance of producing a son before being irretrievably cut out of her father's will. It proved to be another girl.

After this blow they lived between England and Ireland and mostly in debt. The ill-timed births of the two girls, Ettie and Lily, was followed over the next ten years by the belated arrival of three boys, Leland, Ernest and Raymond (called Lee, Ernie and Baa by the family). Emma was incapable of economy both by upbringing and character, and there were continual applications for help to the Langleys and the Walker estates; for in 1871 Tom died of galloping consumption, aged twenty-five, after distinguishing himself as the first man to hit a ball over the old pavilion at Lord's, and winning the Derby. His wife predeceased him and he left a small daughter who inherited his estate and fortune.

Emma's mother, that shadowy figure, simply fades away after her daughter's marriage. Where she lived after Tom came into his inheritance, how she and Emma dealt with each other, whether she ever remarried, and when and where she died are matters that are unknown. Only the inscriptions on the flyleaves of the few books left, the final one, a copy of *Enoch Arden* bearing the words, 'Emma Walker, Ayr, October, 1864', when she was forty-three and her first grandchild was born.

Emma Langley, on the other hand, rose above her misfortunes to judge from the few letters and diaries that survive. We hear of her in the west of Ireland, running the local post office while the postmaster was ill, and extracting as much pleasure from a cottage in which pigs ran about like dogs as she did from high life in Dublin; and of Harry being arrested for whistling 'The Wearing o' the Green' during the troubles, and arriving home after a pleasant evening, ostentatiously removing his boots before getting into bed, to assure Emma that he was sober, and Emma remarking, 'You've forgotten your hat, Harry.' And we also hear of a curious example of precognition on Emma's part, when they were driving in a dog cart along a road in County Cork. She stopped Harry and told him exactly what they would see round the next corner, describing every house, field, haystack and animal. To their amazement it was just as she had said, although they had never been near the place before. At another time Emma had a premonition of danger. She was in the kitchen talking to the cook when one of her children ran in and began playing in front of a large dresser, when Emma, in sudden dread, called the child over to her. A moment later the dresser, which had stood there as long as anyone could remember, fell forward and crashed heavily on the floor. Not being an introspective or easily frightened person she was not disturbed unduly by these events, although they no doubt impressed the cook.

She was an excellent, though eccentric, mother, an inspired nurse when her children were ill, and teacher when they were well, but she had a disastrous tendency to spoil her sons.

The family did not stay in any place for long; Harry would often have to disappear in a hurry, leaving Emma to deal with their creditors and follow on with the children. She was not the sort of person to break under such strains, indeed she was very resilient, but she was deeply unhappy, and it was during this dark period of her life that she and her children were received into the Catholic Church, her conversion, unlike Willie's, coming about through pain. Baa, the youngest of the Langley family was born in 1876, and within a few years, Harry, having provided his wife with five urgent reasons for living, died of consumption.

Emma's position was desperate. Harry left her with no money, and she applied to the trustees of the Walker estate for assistance. After a good deal of hesitation they agreed to make her an allowance of £1,000 a year for life, and Emma settled in Petersham. Her circumstances, her own age and the ages of her children, the exhaustion resulting from the years of insecurity and the illness and death of her husband, all combined to make her about as ineligible a woman as one could find. With five children to provide for and the expenses of a house large enough for them all, and above all, her own inability to manage money, the future must have looked very bleak. She had grown up in a divided house, had thrown away the security and respectability of an arranged marriage by running away with Harry Langley, and had almost immediately begun the long and agonising process of disillusionment.

It was at this juncture in her life that Canon Bagshawe, the parish priest, with rare insight, introduced William Ashford to her.

Eastwood Hall.

Mothers home where she was born. View from Park, looking across the lake. Given me by Mother May 23rd 1905.

Opposite: Two views of Eastwood Hall, near Nottingham, home of the Walkers. The lake has now disappeared and open-cast mining has obliterated the cricket ground.

Above: Bolton Hall, Yorkshire, home of Emma's aunt, Lady Bolton.

Left: Canon Bagshawe of St Elizabeth's church in Richmond

PART III

The Happy Family

———

The attraction between Willie and Emma was instant and strong. Her vitality and wit appealed to him, and her courage in the face of the difficulties that had beset her for so long. Willie's strength of character, integrity and kindness must have drawn Emma as powerfully to him. There was perfect understanding between them from the first.

Before this understanding was generally known Julia wrote a careful note to Willie. 'I do hope you won't be vexed with me for what I am going to say,' she began. 'I did not like to speak to you, because I don't think it fair to worry anyone on the subject . . . I have so often wished, dearest, that you would think of marrying. I do honestly believe it would be for your happiness, and I am sure it would be for the happiness of the one whom you may choose. And it is not as if it need entail our separation. If it *did* I should not urge it,' she admitted frankly, 'because I never could bear *that*. If your wishes point the same way as mine, I can only say that there is every prospect of success.' (Perhaps she had been taken into Emma's confidence.) 'Don't think me meddlesome and interfering,' she went on, 'I only write from the wish to promote your happiness, which is what I have most at heart in this world. And do not be afraid of being teased about it, for I shall never mention the subject to you, unless you speak of it first. God bless you, my own dearest brother . . .'

Nevertheless the prospect of Willie marrying must have begun to recede in her mind as he advanced into middle age, and the likelihood of his now doing so would have been all the more painful.

Expectations of the now aged Maria Ashford's disapproval were high, but she, like Canon Bagshawe, saw at once that Emma would be the perfect wife for Willie, and she gave the match her wholehearted backing. As a product of eighteenth-century parents she found Emma's qualities attractive, and appreciated her robust vitality, her kindness and originality, and her total lack of self-consciousness. Emma must have been

41

considerably relieved at her reception, for even if Maria had liked her personally, the existence of her five children might have made any prospective mother-in-law hesitant.

They were married on 1st July 1880, at St Elizabeth's church at Richmond, Julia being one of the witnesses. The entry for that day in Emma's diary reads, '11 o'clock got married. Willie looked as tho' he were on to a good thing, as no doubt he was. After the breakfast the ladies retired to the drawing room where we all talked good sound sense.'

For their honeymoon they went to Eastwood, not to her old home, for that had been shut since Tom's death, but to her old nurse's cottage in the village, and from there she wrote to Maria.
'My dear Mrs Ashford,

We got here last night and found my old nurse (Old Mary) waiting at the station for us with a carriage and two greys, the driver, who announced himself as "William" and evidently knew me very well, nearly wrung my hand off before I got in, and, I dare not breathe it here, but to this moment I have not the faintest idea who "William" is or was. When we got to Old Mary's cottage there was what she was pleased to term "a humble cup of tea", which consisted of veal cutlets, fried ham, cold tongue, cheesecakes, and hot tea cakes and boiled eggs. Everything so scrupulously clean . . . to-morrow we are to go and see the Bishop of Nottingham and dine with some people here. My late brother's agent called to offer his services . . . and everyone is most kind; and dear Willie seems so thoroughly to enjoy the country, I don't remember ever in my life to have been so perfectly happy.

Fancy leaving all our keys behind us at Richmond, and the day after the wedding Willie had to rush down from London, as there was only one small box we could open when we arrived in town.'

The following day Willie added his assurances, 'It will be long, I trust, before I forget the happy home I have had, but I know you are happy in thinking of my present and (I feel sure) future happiness. We are enjoying our visit very much. Old Mary is doing her utmost to kill us with good living, and Emmie is welcomed among all her old friends.'

They went on into Derbyshire, and it was here that Willie discovered that he had not enough money on him to pay their hotel bill. The banks were shut and the prospect was embarrassing; but Emma, whose past experience enabled her to deal with such a predicament, at once sent him off to the nearest pawnbroker with his gold watch, and they were able to stay another day and redeem the watch before continuing on their journey. Emma also found that she missed her five-year-old son, Baa, and he arrived, accompanied by his nurse, to enjoy the rest of the honeymoon in Derbyshire.

On returning to Petersham they all settled into Elm Lodge, the older Langley boys being sent to school at Prior Park, near Bath. Willie's step-children became extremely fond of him, and he, for his part, looked on them all as his family; they called him 'Father' and he provided them with the affection and security that they had so lamentably missed in their own.

It soon became apparent that the family was to be increased yet further, and the ladies of the house, delighted at the news, began to sew the innumerable garments that the Victorian baby wore, and Julia, being unmarried, was asked by her mother to leave the room whenever any discussion of Emma's pregnancy was imminent. She accepted her dismissal as quite proper, although forty-six by then, so thoroughly had custom in this respect changed since the days of George III.

2 THE ARRIVAL OF DAISY, VERA AND ANGIE

Daisy, christened Margaret Mary Julia, was born in April, 1881, and within a year Emma was pregnant again. But this next child was not to be born at Elm Lodge, because in March, 1882, Maria Ashford died at the age of eighty. The lease of Elm Lodge was not renewed and Willie moved his family to nearby Park Gate, whose charming bow-windowed front is now hidden behind a high brick wall. Here, in November, Vera was born.

The move to Park Gate was a relief to Emma, whose spirit must have chafed living in a house where she was not mistress, and where Julia was

Above left: Willie in the 1870s

Left: Wedding photograph of Emma Langley. 1880

Above: Willie and Emma on their honeymoon, accompanied by Baa and a small dog.

Opposite: A painting by Julian Barrow of Park Gate, Petersham, looking much like it must have when the Ashfords moved there in 1882. Next to it is the churchyard in which lie William, Maria and Julia.
Below: The elegant front of Park Gate, as it is today.

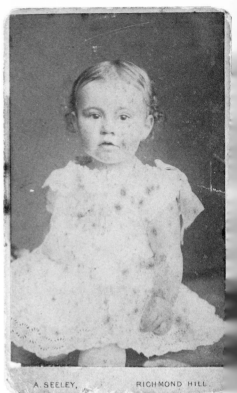

Above: the Ashford family complete at last. Willie and Emma with, *left to right,* Daisy, Angie and Vera.

Right: Daisy aged about 18 months and, *below,* the 'determined' look admired by Julia; Daisy aged 3

always at hand to spoil the infant Daisy. Julia had moved into Byam Cottage, opposite Elm Lodge, taking with her Nana, her old nurse, to look after her. Nana was a temperamental and terrifying Irish woman, completely devoted to Julia, and she drove from the door anyone she considered likely to take advantage of Julia's kind heart, and gave a hearty welcome to visitors of whom she approved.

The removal from Elm Lodge, with its memories of the young Harry, of her parents, and her own youth was painful for Julia. Her feelings for inanimate things and their associations were strong, and in this she differed from Willie who took a more prosaic and unsentimental view. Julia poured out her feelings in a poem, speaking to pictures, furniture and favourite rooms and saying a final farewell to them. She was now, for the first time, on the periphery of the family. She was no longer first in Willie's affections; in the space of two years he had married and her mother had died, and now she had to reconcile herself to living on her own for the first time. It was some comfort that Willie fully appreciated her feelings, and treated her with more than his usual kindness and affection; and that Emma, though not sensitive, understood the depth of the relationship between brother and sister, and had the wisdom to accept it.

The reduction in Julia's circumstances, which necessitated her moving to such a small house, must have come as a shock at her time of life. The house contained two bedrooms, an attic with a tiny balcony, a kitchen, dining room and sitting room. In the little garden to the side she kept chickens and tended a small vegetable patch. She could have people to stay but numbers had to be limited. Willie and Emma, after their move to Sussex, often came, singly or together, and a bed was made up of pillows for whichever of the children accompanied them. When alone Julia lived in the upmost simplicity. She was scrupulous about money and one of her letters begins, 'Thank you for sending on my gloves and I enclose 6d for the postage.'

However, the arrival of her two nieces was a source of particular happiness to her and she continued to dote on them and to find fresh evidence of their remarkable qualities at every visit. In 1884 another daughter, Angela (Angie), was born, the last and favourite of Emma's children, and twenty years younger than Ettie. There was, inevitably, a certain amount of jealousy from the two Langley girls, but Willie's un-wavering tact and affection went a great way to soothing their feelings.

3   AUNTIE'S JEWEL AND FATHER MCSWINEY

Angie and Vera were the only ones out of eight children not to inherit Emma's dark eyes; Vera's were grey and Angie's blue. All three sisters had fair hair when they were very young, Daisy's darkening to a beautiful golden brown later. A photograph of her aged three sitting on a studio rock and holding one shoe in her hand, shows a round and very determined face. A story of her at about this age confirms her determination. Julia, for whom such errands were a special treat, took Daisy out shopping, for Daisy had announced that she wanted a pair of pink shoes. The assistant in the shop was most helpful, but pink shoes, then, as now, were not common. She produced every shade of red, at which Daisy invariably and calmly remarked, 'They're not pink'. Julia tried other shops with the same result, and at last began to try and persuade her to consider other colours, but Daisy only said, 'I want *pink* shoes,' and in the end was brought apologetically home by her aunt without any at all. Emma in similar circumstances would soon have lost patience and bought shoes of another colour, for she did not believe in pandering to her children's fads.

Vera, a year younger than Daisy, was a typical Ashford child with her grey eyes and fair hair which later became quite dark, and she was her father's favourite. She had the same fearless spirit as Emma and from the first there was a special bond between them. All three sisters loved and feared their mother, but they idolised their father; when they were older they teased and spoiled him, asked his advice, quoted his opinions and leaped to his defence. He was never angry with them, but they dreaded his disapproval.

Daisy naturally was the first to receive letters from Julia. They were usually written in the third person, always easier for a young child to understand, and she evidently saw no reason to relax her high standards, for her letters to Daisy are faultlessly formal throughout. She was, however, lavish in her endearments; Daisy was always 'Auntie's Jewel of the World', 'Auntie's Pet' and must have '10,000 kisses from her Old Auntie'. Daisy absorbed these extravagances like a sponge, and would dictate her replies to either of her parents, for both were ready to take down verbatim what their three-year-old daughter dictated. An example of Daisy's precocity is a letter written from Bath where she had gone with her parents to visit the older Langley boys at school. Addressed to Julia and written in Emma's lop-sided handwriting, it is dated 11th April 1884, only four days after Daisy's third birthday.

'*9 Duke St.*

Bath.

Dear Auntie,

I'm writing a letter for dear Auntie . . . I like you so much. Dear Auntie I love you very much & dear Auntie I like you. Auntie; Daisy & Papa & Mama sleep in Mama's room, same room as father's & as mine; onpacking some ties father was yesterday. I can't be rocked now 'cos I'm 3. I go to sleep wizout rocking all by myself. Good morning Auntie, I like you so much [she continues, surely to Julia's intense gratification]. '*There was a priest died in my church & Mother says I may go in if I liked. He died a long time ago. I'm warming a pocky hanky, one of Mother's, I'm getting it up 3 times – I'm ondoing it & I'm fixing it.*

There was a little boy at Prior Park & some big boy knocked him down & there was a roller there right at the bottom of the hill. He's dead, dead now, a roller killed him . . .

I've a lot of words to tell Auntie & she is a very good girl, dear Auntie that's so good to Daisy – that's all.

With Papa's best love & his head & his towdowders I remain a good woman. You're a good woman and Father's a good gekleum,

from

Daydums'

1884

Dear Auntie

I'm writing a letter for dear
Auntie I write a boodly letter for you
I like you so much. Dear Auntie
I love you very much & dear
Auntie I like you. Auntie; Daisy
& Papa & Mama sleep in Mama's
room, same room as father's 2 a
mine; onpacking some ties father
was yesterday. I can't be rock
now 'cos I'm 3. I go to sleep

Daisy aged about 4

Daisy's earliest letter written, in spite of the Park Gate address,
from Bath.

Opposite: Vera aged 3 and Daisy, 4

BYRNE & C°   HILL STREET,

In another letter, also in Emma's hand, Daisy describes a visit to the circus. 'Daisy saw a man in black velvet and scarlet sleeves riding on a horse, and Daisy laughed so very much, and Daisy said "Wasn't the circus lovely", and the elephants danced on the tubs and Daisy said, "Oh how nice the circus is" '. And in another letter she transforms a walk in the park, when a small dog had run out of some bushes and barked at her, into, 'Daisy was out walking to-day when a big lion jumped out and bit your Little Jewel.' Julia, of course, was all sympathy.

Birthdays and Chrismas were commemorated by Julia in verse:

'Love thrones in Margaret's dark brown eyes,
Peace shines from Vera's orbs of grey,
While Joy at Hide and Seek doth play
In Angela's, blue as the skies.'

In 1885, when Daisy was still only four, a Jesuit priest, Father McSwiney, came to stay at Park Gate. Daisy was fascinated by him and was discovered hiding under her father's desk in his study, the better to overhear their conversation. When he had gone she told Willie that she wanted to write his Life, and Willie, taking paper and pen, sat down at his desk and told her to begin right away. So with hands clasped behind her back, she walked up and down the room and dictated an entirely fictitious biography of four thousand words. It was an extraordinary effort for a child of her age; the narrative flows, Father McSwiney's saintly boyhood is described, and the Pope is depicted at the railway station at Barnes 'trying his weight' while waiting for a train to take him to London to see the sights. At one point the handwriting changes to Emma's, and then back again to Willie's, so there must have been several dictating sessions before Father McSwiney is left in monkish se-clusion at Manresa House in Roehampton. Daisy's parents, of course, found it highly amusing, but not very surprising, and the manuscript was put carefully away. While they encouraged enterprise and talent they did nothing to force it, and Daisy's was allowed to grow at its own pace.

Whenever she was allowed to, Julia took Daisy to call on friends and relatives and any praise of her darling was retailed to Willie and Emma;

how her 'pretty and clever looks' had appealed to one, or 'her little air of determination' to another. She could not afford to buy expensive presents, but she made her clothes and sent her pictures, and ribbons for her dolls, and in return Daisy learned to knit and presented her aunt with red woollen ear-muffs which she insisted on Julia wearing all the time she was with her.

4 EMMA

Emma entered with characteristic zest into the cultivated atmosphere that surrounded Willie and Julia. Though with no literary pretensions herself, she too wrote verses; not the eighteenth century kind full of classical allusions that Julia produced, but brisk lines, larded with slang and a knockabout humour. She could dash off whole letters in verse and could never resist inscribing the books she gave away as presents. The more inappropriate the verse the better she was pleased. In a religious book she gave Julia in 1887 she wrote:

> 'To my dear sister, Julia,
> I present this book peculiar:
> Though somewhat deep, it is not low,
> And it's all by Father Antonio.
> It is a Christmas box from me,
> Your very affectionate sister, E.'

She ended a verse letter to Daisy:

> 'Goodbye, my darling little child,
> Do not be rude or mad or wild.
> If Auntie says, "Come hither," come,
> And do not stand and suck your thumb,
> And when she says, "Get out," why, go,
> And I'm your own old loving Mo.'

Mo was their name for her when they were small, and their father they called Pops. On the flyleaf of *The Fifteen Decisive Battles of the World* which she gave Willie she wrote simply, 'From a dark woman of much discretion,' and in two volumes of Thackeray, a great favourite of Willie's,

> 'This little tribute, sir, I bring
> And at thy grand old feet I fling.
> It shows the love of a sterling wife
> Who treads with thee the path of life.'

and underneath she added, 'Quotations from unpublished works of the Early Fathers.'

Emma was, too, a great reader; she loved the novels of the day, and when the girls were older she read Dickens aloud to them, skipping the dull passages, and infecting her listeners with her own enjoyment. Poetry she also read, particularly Scott and Tennyson, whose narrative writing appealed to her. Byron, of course, had not yet emerged from under his cloud, and the classicism of Keats and Shelley and their passionate sensitivity were not to her taste.

She herself taught the children to read and write, and she must have begun early, for Daisy could not remember a time when she was unable to read. She told them stories, too, from the Bible, describing the characters as though they were known personally to her: Jacob resting after the day's work wore on his head, according to Emma, a red, spotted handkerchief, knotted at the corners.

A dictation book that belonged to Daisy contains earnest poems such as:

> 'Hearts good and true
> Have wishes few
> In narrow circles bounded,
> And hope that lives
> On what God gives
> Is Christian hope well founded.'

followed immediately by, 'Oh sharper than a serpent's thanks it is to have a toothless child.' And a thoughtful sentence about Edward IV and his regrettable love of pleasure is followed by a paragraph about 'The Mother': 'What a grand and noble idea is the mother. Without her children would be conspicuous by their absence. The song says, "What is home without a mother?" and we reply, "A delusion and a snare, several degrees worse than a mother without a home, to whom we would suggest the Union".'

'The Father' also came in for comment: 'The British Father is a grand creature, much respected by the nobility and gentry. He is popularly supposed to be the breadwinner, but sometimes he prefers that someone else should procure the bread and he eats it. From this you will gather that the Father has his good points, and he is nothing if he is not accommodating.' The sight of her small daughters bent solemnly over their dictation must have added considerably to Emma's pleasure.

For music she preferred ballads and the Scots and Irish airs she had learned as a child from her mother. For these she had a real love, which she passed on to her children, who remembered them all their lives.

Like the Ashfords, she was an enthusiastic theatre goer, and anniversaries and birthdays were usually celebrated by a trip to London to see a play or one of the Gilbert and Sullivan operas. In 1883 the Ashfords gave a Fancy Dress party for which they took over the school hall, and Emma afterwards wrote a limerick about each guest, fifty-four in number, which she had printed under the title of *A Fancy Ballad*. All the Langley children were present, Baa, her youngest son, being then seven.

5 THE MOVE TO LEWES

In 1889 the whole family went to the Isle of Wight for a holiday, and one afternoon Daisy and Vera wandered off along the road without anyone seeing them. They were soon attracted by the sound of voices, and they turned in at a gate and found themselves on a wide lawn on which a garden party was in progress. A man detached himself from the crowd and approached them, and after talking to them politely for a minute he asked them whether they would care for an ice cream. They were drawn into the circle of guests and made much of, and supplied not only with ice cream but with cakes as well. Their new-found friend was very attentive and told them, among other things, that he was the king of the island (this was in a sense true – Prince Henry of Battenburg became Governor of the Isle of Wight in 1889). Daisy was impressed, but Vera was outraged and said, 'No, you're not, Father is.' At this awkward moment their father himself appeared on his bicycle, rather hot and very anxious, and immediately, to Vera's annoyance, took off his hat to their host and addressed him as 'sir'.

In the same year the Ashfords moved away from Petersham, ostensibly to escape the damp and enervating air of the Thames valley. The real reason for the decision was Emma's wish to remove her children from the indulgence of their aunt. Julia spoiled and petted them, and, living so near, was always calling. She was also involved in the same parish and musical activities as Willie, which meant frequent consultations with him. It would have required a good deal more patience than Emma possessed not to find her constant presence irritating. Though very fond of her sister-in-law, Emma had had enough.

The place they chose was Lewes, and they took a lease on a large Victorian house in St Anne's Crescent, overlooking the valley of the Ouse, and in the path of the bracing winds by which Emma set such store. Transporting a family of ten, with servants and luggage and furniture, was an exhausting business and they stayed at the White Hart hotel while the house was made ready for them. 'If you really want to lose friends recommend them to stay here,' Emma noted bitterly in her diary.

Southdown House, now the headquarters of the county library, still stands, hideous and grey, on the hillside, its front, facing north, only a yard or two back from the pavement, and the front door approached up a short flight of steps. But so steep is the hill on which it is built that the ground floor becomes the first floor when viewed from the garden at the rear of the house, and the height of the whole building is considerable. In the Ashfords' day there were stone steps leading up into the hall from the garden, and greenhouses to one side. From the windows at the back can be seen the Downs, which rise sharply on the far side of the river and on which light and shadow make constant play; and below and to the left of the house the town falls away into the valley. This was the house remembered most vividly by the three sisters as the home of their childhood. The rooms have large windows and high ceilings, and an unusual feature of the house is the single staircase that rises from the basement to the top storey; there were no back stairs.

They were delighted with the move. The Catholic church of St Pancras was only a few minutes' walk from the house, near enough for the young Ashfords and Langleys often to arrive late for Mass. And an old friend, Father McAuliffe, was parish priest, a saintly and much loved man. Lewes itself was an Assize town, with the judge's stately processions to and from the Court, and, once, a Catholic judge attended Mass before an awed congregation; Catholic churches were not used to such civic manifestations. Then there was the Corn Exchange, scene of Buffalo Bill's travelling show where the whole family thrilled to the Deadwood stage being attacked by Indians and rescued by the colonel and his sharp-shooters. There was the old castle and the ruins of the eleventh-century Priory of St Pancras. And on 5th November the annual noisy march through the town took place with the Guy to be burned on the bonfire. This was considered too rough and rowdy an occasion for the children to be allowed out of doors to see, and in any case there was always a strong current of anti-Catholic feeling among the marchers. On the Downs, strings of elegant racehorses were to be seen taking their exercise, and, for the children, the steep bare hills, with houses nestling in the hollows and sheep grazing over the heights, were an endless source of adventure.

Vera, in a memoir she wrote many years later, said, 'The day nursery was a delightful room that gave a view across the levels to the Downs. There was one break in the line of hills where on fine days we could see the crane working at Newhaven harbour, and on wet, watch the sea mists rolling in and gradually covering the Downs with white cotton-woolly caps.'

Been up + down here 1000's of times.

Lewes. High Street.

MEZOTINT CO YORK HILL LONDON ROAD BRIGHTON

St. Ann's Hill + our church many times we have been in late years. Our photos taken by Lucy. Oct. 18th 1904 the day Bishop Amega paid his 1st visit. St Ann's church we have been to for a wedding + the church yard for painting + several funerals.

From the collection of postcards
Vera made before sadly leaving
Lewes in 1904

+ I pushed Angie in when we were children + she got covered with duckweed + was soaked. We have had many trudges up to the windmills + runs down the hill with the path.

WINTERBOURNE
LEWES

COPYRIGHT

Left: Southdown House, Lewes. The bay window on the left at the rear of the house was the day nursery where Daisy wrote.

Above: The garden steps at Southdown House, 1891. From the top: Algy Petre and Willie, Emma with Angie, Vera and Daisy.

Below: Seaford, scene of many picnics for the Ashford children

If the day was fine Emma used to interrupt lessons in the day nursery and send the children out for long walks with the governess, or down to the station to catch a train to Seaford, where they could picnic and bathe. They must be out of doors as much as possible and any unwholesome interest in health or any tendency to prefer the house to the garden was stamped on at once.

Daisy was nine, Vera eight and Angie six when they moved from Petersham. Daisy enjoyed her special status as the eldest; it was she who decided what games to play, she who began Latin lessons with her father, she who received letters addressed to Miss Ashford, while her sisters remained 'Miss V.' and 'Miss A.' Ashford. Vera, who later became the stronger personality, occasionally quarrelled with Daisy, but their mutual affection made these quarrels of short duration. All their lives Daisy and Vera were the closest of the three sisters.

6 THE LANGLEYS AND THE 'THOUGHT BOYS'

When they had settled into Southdown House Daisy and Vera began doing lessons with a governess while Angie played with her dolls or went for walks with her nurse. But Emma would often whisk her favourite away to Brighton to return with a new dress or hat, and Daisy and Vera, filled with envy, would feign indifference or worse when Angie triumphantly displayed them. Poor Angie, guileless all her life, was always disappointed at their reaction to her good fortune, and Emma was oblivious to the trouble she caused her favourite daughter.

The Langley boys were almost grown up when the family moved to Lewes. They were only at home during the holidays, and as they left school they began to lead their own lives. Leland, who was very musical and had a fine voice, was told that he should study singing in Italy, and Emma persuaded Willie to stand the cost. Willie could never resist her persuasions, just as Emma herself could never resist the demands of her sons.

Ernest, on leaving school, joined Frank Benson's Shakespeare company, his chief qualification being that he was a very good rugger player, for Benson, a sportsman himself, liked to be able to play local clubs as the company toured the country. He spent several years on stage and rugger pitch and later went to seek his fortune in the gold mines of South Africa. Before he left England, Willie offered some financial help but Ernest, to his credit, said, 'I've got two hands, and I'm perfectly fit, and if I can't make a living I'm not worth much.' And off he went. Baa, when he had left school, joined Leland in London where he appeared in a few minor roles on the stage. Later he became a confirmed gambler and his fortunes rose and fell at the many race meetings he attended. He once pulled off a historic racing coup. He forecast the winners, well in advance, of the six classic doubles and at enormous odds, finishing with the November handicap. Before this race he asked for the prayers of a convent in Dublin and the nuns, truly Irish, were almost as jubilant as Baa when his horse won. He himself fainted as it passed the winning post.

Ettie and Lily lived at home, watching their brothers come and go and their small, lively stepsisters take up much of their mother's time. To make matters worse for them they did not even get on with each other, and were continually at loggerheads. Ettie was outspoken and tactless, affectionate and independent, too like Emma for comfort in the same house. And Lily, romantic and temperamental to a degree, was devoted to her mother. But she quarrelled easily and was usually not on speaking terms with at least one member of the family; her feuds might last for months at a time and end as inexplicably as they had begun. She was a martyr to her brothers' teasing, but had generally enough humour to withstand it. Her influence on her stepsisters when they were children was greater than Ettie's, and when she wanted to punish them for something she told them to refuse second helpings at lunch time when they often joined their parents in the dining room. When Emma offered them more of their favourite pudding Lily had only to give them a glance and there was a chorus of 'No, thank you, Mother.' Emma never suspected the reason for their saying 'no' and it never occurred to the children to tell her or their father why they had refused. They were very fond of Lily for all that, and she enjoyed their company, always taking an interest in what they were doing and entering into their games when asked. She was a splendid mimic, as were all three little girls, and she entertained them by the hour with accounts of her 'Thought Boys', an imaginary family whose voices and mannerisms she embellished at every telling. They were, being Lily's inventions, a mixture of the romantic and the eccentric, and so popular did they become that even her brothers and their friends could sometimes persuade her to 'tell'. One of her characters was a revolting, smug little boy in a velvet suit, called Cedric Denis Vere Colemayne, 4th Viscount Ennis. This child was always amazed when he met anyone who had not heard of him and used to say, 'Don't you *know*? Haven't you *heard*?' And even worse, he called his mother '*Madre mia*'. Lily's sisters entreated her to kill off this monster, but she kept him alive through many instalments.

To a lessser degree Daisy, Vera and Angie had their own 'Thought Boys' – their dolls, who, in Vera's and Angie's case, were members of the aristocracy. Vera was the Duchess of Roxburgh and Angie the Duchess of Northumberland, and their dolls were their children. They happily married off these creations, sent them to war, nursed them when they were wounded, presented their daughters at court, and in general made them lead full and interesting lives. 'No other children we knew,' Vera remembered, 'ever quite entered into our games with dolls . . . What other children could understand the perpetual worry that Angie's James and my John couldn't possibly go into the same regiment? My father used to be pestered by us both in turn and to almost every suggestion would come, "Oh, but Father, my John has blue eyes and fair hair, so he couldn't possibly go into a regiment with red facings." Or "Not into a heavy dragoon regiment, he's quite thin." Nothing would ever convince us that a heavy regiment didn't mean one entirely composed of fat men.'

Daisy, by contrast, had a working-class family. The Ashford word for this was 'mere', and the mother of this family was known as 'mere Mrs Ham', played by Daisy with aggravating relish. Mrs Ham lived at 15 Devonshire Road, Petersfield, Hants., and her husband wore a peaked cap with brass lettering round it. He returned nightly from his work at

Vera, Daisy and Angie. 1891

'The Portsmouth Naval Works' with very dirty hands. On Saturday nights Mrs Ham's daughters, Ethel and Ella, had their hair done up in tight pigtails, to be really 'crimpy' for Sunday. Vera and Angie were fascinated by the Hams, but sometimes Daisy would stand with her hands on her hips and make rude remarks, in the role of Mrs Ham, about the ducal offspring in the middle of a levée or a garden party. 'In deadly retaliation,' Vera continues, 'Angie and I took our revenge by bestowing our children's cast-off clothing on Daisy's children, and the more unsuitable this was to their humble station the more satisfying our revenge. "Very well, if you *will* be such a beast, I will give your Ethel a most beautiful white silk accordion pleated dress with everything to match," was a crushing retort calculated to wound Mrs Ham's deepest feelings. Daisy blissfully sailed along planting her children out happily in the world as grocers' boys and gardeners etc. Truly an easygoing existence.'

They all three envied what Vera called 'The divine liberty of the children of the streets'. 'It filled the two duchesses no less than Mrs Ham with envy,' she wrote. 'Why couldn't we play hopscotch on the red brick pavements? Why not rush out with our tea (a large hunk of bread and jam) in our hands, untroubled by plates or the injunctions to "Sit up and don't stoop", "Don't kick the table", "Don't get down till everyone has finished"? These were questions no grown-up ever answered to our satisfaction.'

7 THE WRITING OF 'THE YOUNG VISITERS'

It was within a year of the move to Lewes that Daisy embarked on the book that made her famous, but already behind her were three stories all dictated to her father: *The Life of Father McSwiney*, previously mentioned, *Mr Chapmer's Bride* (among the lost manuscripts), and *A Short Story of Love and Marriage*, written when she was eight. This last title is indeed an exact description of the book, the first of its two chapters being called 'Love' and the second 'Marriage'. Of the three most important events in human experience birth, to children, is by far the most interesting, but in Daisy's case this was shrouded in Victorian secrecy. In the experience of the Ashford girls weddings were a time for open jollity and endless chat both before and after the celebrations. Daisy listened attentively and observed closely on such occasions, and the result is two hilarious chapters. Her descriptions, even of heroes and heroines, is dispassionate and clinical. 'Mr Molvern,' she states, 'was a red haired quick tempered gentleman with very small grey eyes and a clever looking pink face.' The conversation, of which there is a great deal, combines, in a delightful way, adult phraseology and childish thought. The story concerns a young man, Burke, keen enough for his truelove's company, but curiously reluctant to marry her. When cornered by Edith on the subject, he says, 'You must recollect that I am not a good dancer and have no nice suits, and you must recollect my people are not in this neighbourhood and I can't write marriage letters . . . and I don't think my people would like me to be married just yet as I am not quite twenty-nine.' Edith, undaunted by these feeble excuses, presses him further until he declares, 'Look here, I wish you would talk of something else. I have a good mind not to marry you at all.' However, he does relent and Daisy's account of the wedding and the clothes worn by the bridal couple and the guests is minute. Willie's self-control as he filled page after page with Daisy's prose must be admired. The slightest faltering on his part, the faintest suggestion of a smile, might have meant an instant halt to the narrative.

The Young Visiters, written in her own hand in 1890 when she was nine, shows an extraordinary development of her talent; her observation is more acute, she is confident in her use of words and the construction of chapters. There is not the repetition and occasional wildness of *A Short Story of Love and Marriage*. She has become aware of social distinctions, of that distant, gay and brilliant world of London society, and of the sort of anxieties to be endured by a humble man ambitious to enter it.

Mr Salteena's adventures take up most of the book and Daisy is merciless in describing his frequent humiliations and disappointments in his attempts to enter society. We suffer with him even while we laugh; the indignity of having no knee-breeches for the levée at Buckingham Palace,

Daisy aged about 10

Below: Pages from the original manuscript of *The Young Visiters*

Opposite: Daisy, aged 9, with a favourite doll

Chap 10th
Preparing for the fray
___

The next few days were indeed bussy for Ethel and Bernard. First of all Ethel got some dainty pink note paper with silver crest on it and sent out invitations in the following terms to all their friends.

Miss Ethel Monticue will be married to Mr Bernard Clark at Westminster Abbey on June 10th. Your company is requested there at 2-30 sharp and afterwards for refreshment at the Gaiety Hotel R. S. V. P.

Having posted heaps of these and got several replies Ethel began to order her wedding dress which cost a good bit. She chose a rich satin with a humped pattern of gold on the pure white and it had a long train edged with tirum lilies. Her veil was of pure lace with a crown of orange blossom. Her bauquett she ordered to be of white dog daisies St Joseph lilies and orange blossams tied up with pale blue satin ribbon — You will indeed be a charming spectacle my darling gasped Bernard at their

and of being told to roll up his trousers as no one will notice; his awkwardness over tipping a maid; his becoming 'flustered with his forks' at dinner; even his excitement over having early morning tea in bed. He is only sustained by the hope that one day he will find all these things quite commonplace, and by the sheer exhilaration of mixing with the aristocracy. Inexorably, however, Daisy puts him in his place. He loses Ethel and marries instead the inferior Bessie Topp with her 'round red face and rather stary eyes'. And although he achieves his ambition of galloping after the Prince of Wales' barouche, Daisy, implacable to the last, gives him an unruly horse whose mane he is obliged to clutch. He is referred to throughout the book as Mr Salteena, although the heroine is always Ethel and the man she falls in love with, Bernard. Perhaps she felt that she should not be too familiar with 'an elderly man of 42'.

The child's own recent experiences are recorded: Ethel is shown wearing a blue frock which had 'grown rarther short in the sleeves'; and the child gives her characters what she herself would like, 'jam tarts with plenty of jam in them' or 'rarther nice sweets which stuck to his teeth'. Noticing people did not talk at parties as they talked among their own families, she refers to the 'socierty tone' used by Ethel, whose conversation echoes the nursery wrangles between the sisters as well as the provocative bickering of Ettie and Lily.

The story is unfolded effortlessly and with a mature richness of vocabulary. She had learned to draw her minor characters with a few brief strokes and she fills in the background in a masterly way that does not distract the reader from the main drama. She drew some of her characters from the succession of friends and relatives who came to the house for extended visits; eccentric cousins at whom one must not laugh, grave elderly clerics, gay young racing and acting friends of her stepbrothers, who came under Emma's powerful spell.

The Young Visiters, in its twopenny exercise book, was read by her parents and put away with the collection of children's writings and drawings, and lay forgotten until it was rediscovered nearly thirty years later among Emma's papers.

8 PARENTS AND STEPSISTERS

Emma was not unduly house-proud, nor was she much interested in fancy cooking. As long as the food was wholesome, that was all she asked. The lease of the house, which cost Willie £80 a year, included an orchard and garden on the other side of the road and he let this to a man on condition that he supplied them with fruit and vegetables. Emma herself was a keen gardener and took charge of the greenhouses and their own large garden. She ran the house with energy, more concerned with the inhabitants than with the house itself, but she would not tolerate slovenly work. In pursuit of an erring maid or a naughty child the sound of her footsteps ascending or descending the stairs in a purposeful manner was enough to warn everyone of her displeasure. Servants would wonder what they had left undone and the children in the nursery would leap hastily back into bed and feign sleep.

She did not, as has been seen, leave the upbringing of her children to other people; she liked to have them round her. She helped to put them to bed, and she heard their prayers. From an early age they often joined their parents for lunch in the dining room. Willie also enjoyed their company in the library and he sometimes took them to watch cricket matches in Brighton, or accompanied them on their walks. He talked to them as though they were his contemporaries, and his pleasure and surprise in finding himself a father seemed to endure to the end of his life. The result of all this was that the children never regarded nurses or governesses as substitute parents, nor did they give them the extravagant and pathetic affection so often described in biographies of the period.

The engaging of servants, that source of so many Victorian and Edwardian jokes, Emma found very tedious, and she sometimes left the choice to Lily, who, on one occasion when Emma was away from home, engaged as butler an undersized boy with a hoarse, Irish voice, freckles and spiky red hair, whose name was Johnny. Lily had had qualms about

69

Johnny's suitability and also his ability to carry heavy trays upstairs, but he had assured her earnestly, 'I'm very strong, miss', and she had succumbed to his charm. Emma was both horrified and amused on seeing her new butler, but at Lily's pleading she allowed him to stay until she could replace him. He did his best, too, though being so small, he found handing round the dishes at table very difficult. It was only when he was discovered weeping on the stairs that Emma decided that he had to go.

Father McAuliffe used to recommend servants to her, but they were often men who had just been released from Lewes prison, and depending on their crimes, they were accepted or rejected. Willie left such arrangements entirely to Emma, although he must frequently have found it inconvenient to remember which of the household had a prison record. Johnny was followed by Alfredo, another butler who was discovered in tears, though in his case they were brought about by nostalgia for his native land on hearing Leland singing in Italian one evening after dinner.

In arranging the furniture at Southdown House Emma was swayed more by passing fashions and inventions than by any aesthetic ideas. She had no taste. Her children remembered her removing a set of Sheraton dining room chairs and replacing them with heavy and hideous ones to which she had taken a fancy. Like Vera later in life, she could not resist gadgets, and an armchair that could be transformed at the pressing of a lever into a sort of bulbous *chaise-longue* appealed strongly to her and she bought it. Willie seems never to have objected to her innovations and it is a temptation to suppose that he was somewhat under his wife's thumb. However, this would be wrong. Like Julia he lived an intense spiritual and intellectual life, and the idea of interfering in domestic matters would simply not have occurred to him. If Emma was happy then so was he, and they understood and appreciated each other very well. Appeals to him by his daughters when Emma had bought them clothes they detested were met with, 'Your mother knows best'. And they had to endure wearing black and white striped stockings, which Emma thought pretty but which the children of Lewes found extremely funny, prickly serge dresses with huge collars and floppy sleeves, and hats unlike any that were worn by their friends. To add to their misery at such times

Emma would insist on them having their photographs taken, when they stared, glum and despairing, into the lens for posterity. It was her insensitivity that had played a large part in Emma's ability to survive her early struggles.

At fifty she was as zestful as ever, enjoying society, theatre-going and presiding over her large family. She enjoyed life and saw no reason why other people should not do likewise. She made no particular effort to find husbands for Ettie and Lily because she had had no difficulty in that direction herself, and she probably put down their spinsterhood to choice rather than to lack of opportunity.

In 1893 Ettie was nearing thirty and, unable to support the idea of spending the rest of her life at home, she took a post as governess in an Italian family and spent some years in Italy. A few months after her arrival she wrote an affectionate letter to Willie for his birthday from Vaioni, 'My dearest old Father, I do hope you will get this on the morning of the 24th to wish you many happy returns of the day.' She apologises for being unable to send his present until the following week, 'My consolation,' she adds, 'being in the fact that I feel sure you will be just as pleased with my wish to send you something as if it came in time.' This insight into Willie's character is followed by a long account of a pilgrimage she made to Montenero, a shrine high up in the mountains, a combination of physical perseverence and spiritual benefit that she knew would interest him.

Lily, jealous of Ettie's enterprise, decided that she, too, would become a governess, and she went to teach English in Poland. She returned, however, after only a few months, in a state of high dudgeon, having quarrelled with her employers, and having acquired a strong Polish accent that it took the combined efforts of her three brothers to eradicate. Of Emma's eight children Lily was the most difficult. She could be an amusing companion, but she was malicious, and was adept at making mischief between different members of the family. Before her departure for Poland Willie had been driven to remark as he said goodbye that he hoped she would improve before returning home, and this, from Willie, was strong talk. Although Lily was so devoted to her, Emma seems to

Ten year old Vera
wearing the hated striped stockings

Daisy (sitting) and Angie
in their new serge dresses

Right: Julia, the beloved aunt,
as an old woman

have had little influence on her. The person who was usually able to take the sting out of her by making her laugh was her youngest brother, Baa. He had a happy sense of the ridiculous and was, besides, very fond of his sister. It was he who adopted a Polish accent even stronger than hers, seconded by Leland and Ernest; he who teased Lily about imaginary lovers, and listened delightedly to stories of her Thought Boys. His attention must have been balm to this destructive woman.

9 JULIA, THE PERFECT AUNT

A frequent visitor to Southdown House was Julia, approaching sixty, but as alert and interested in life as ever, and always ready to be bullied by her nieces. In the early nineties she was engaged on the translation from the French of *The Life of Saint Philip Benizi*, which necessitated a visit to Paris, which she had not seen since 1855. Willie's opinion and advice were often sought on such matters and he himself, at this time, was making his own translation of *The Manual of Liturgiology*.

Daisy and her sisters were frequent visitors to Byam Cottage, accompanied by either parent or by Lily or Ettie. Nana, who allowed them to shell peas or feed the chickens for her, was as strict with them as Julia was soft. Vera, waving at the butcher's boy from the window, found herself in Nana's bad books, accused of familiarity. Julia took them on afternoon calls to Ham House and to her many friends in Petersham, and over the river to cousins in Twickenham. Sometimes they visited Berkeley Square, where an ageing but hospitable cousin lived in style, and where they were awed by the magnificent footmen. Daisy was especially popular with her elderly relations and Julia could never show her off enough.

When separated from each other correspondence was kept up between them, that from Lewes often in the form of begging letters. 'My darling Auntie,' began Vera soon after the move to Sussex, 'I am so sorry that I have not written to you for such a long time, but I have got some secret and important things to tell you so I will write you a pretty long letter.

First, do you know, dear Auntie, that I shall have to take 5 or 6 shillings out for the birthdays that are coming? Father's comes 1st. I think I am going to get him a nice tobacco pouch and I am going to get a pound or so of Dark Virginia to put in it, so I expect that alone will cost 2/-. Then comes Angie's birthday. Now this is the most secret thing of all so don't let it out please. Well! I am going to give her a rabit. The other evening when she and I were alone she came over to me and said, "Vera," she said, "What are you going to give me for a birthday present?" So I said to her, "Quiriosity killed a cat." So she said, "Oh, Vera darling, do give me an alive animal." So I said, "Well, my dear, I'll see. I can't promise anything yet." So I spoke to Mother about it going to church last Wednesday and Mother consented and I am going down this evening to Joe Kings to see if I cant get a ribbit hutch. I think he'd let me have a second hand one for about 1/6 and I shall get a 1/6 rabit of the woman at the Priory ruins if she will sell me one for that. I expect she will,' continued Vera confidently, 'when I tell her that I am paying for it out of my own money. If there is any money over I shall get a yard or so of cambrick to make my two dolls Sunday dresses. My darling Queen, could you send me 2 yards of pale blue ribbon and 2 yards of pink. I shall not know how to thank you if you do. It is twelve o'clock,' she adds piously, 'and the Angelus is ringing. I must say them . . . I have said them, and I have said them for you dear Auntie. I am your very affectionate niece Vera.'

Julia responded as an Aunt should, and the resulting rabbit marked the beginning of Angie's career as a fancier. It was also, Vera maintained all her life, the most appreciated present she ever gave, and certainly the one she most enjoyed giving. Angie tended her rabbit with meticulous care and when she had bought a mate for it she joined the Lewes Rabbit Fanciers' Association in order to exhibit them at the annual show. When the time for the show arrived she took her pets down to the Corn Exchange where it was to take place and left them there. But on returning later, accompanied by a nervous maid, she discovered, to her fury, that her rabbits were not in the most prominent position. In spite of protests from the maid who was inclined to think that the committee knew best,

Angie burst in on the astonished members, loudly demanding a better place for her rabbits, and so eloquent and persistent was she that they agreed to rearrange the hutches to suit her. When she was satisfied her anger subsided and she returned home cheerfully. Her outburst seems out of character, for as she grew up she became extremely shy and self-effacing.

Another letter from Vera to Julia begins, 'Pax take 'em dear Auntie,' but in spite of the opening this is not a begging letter. They were always on the lookout for extra cash as an undated letter from Daisy shows – as there were no coming birthdays with which to wring Julia's heart she was reduced to writing:

My Angel Auntie.
I am writing you a very short but important business letter. It is not private. You know that I am a member of the 'Hagat Writing board' . . . so I am writing for your subscription for the Writing board – it is only 6d and a shilling under extremely exaggerated terms, so with kind regards I am

Head member of the Hagat Writing board
(Daisy)

But Julia was not only a source of income; her opinion was often sought on literary matters. Two surviving poems of Vera's were sent off and returned with comments on both in Julia's neat hand:

A poor girl at Night
It was so dark at midnight
The London streets were bere,
When a poor child came in sight
It was so very clear

PART II
Her bleeding feet were durty
Her hands were durty too
I felt so very sorry
It throb me through and through.

PART III

Oh God, take pity on her
Who had no home to warm her
And everyone forgot her
That night in London Town.
End

The Clods

Ah beautiful clouds
Roling on
Never stoping and never gone
Rain and sunshine
The clods role on.

On the following page was written in large letters, 'For what Auntie thinks of them', and Julia had replied, 'Old Auntie likes Wara's "pomes" very much indeed. The story of the poor girl nearly made her cry. The lines on the clouds are lovely.'

Another piece that has survived, torn from a note book, and entitled A Rainy Day, was the joint effort of Daisy and Vera, and probably an essay on a subject given by Emma or their governess. 'I like a rainy day except it makes the earth wet and flaby. Nurses are allways cross on wet days that you feel you could go to sleep. You feel your chest is alive and is thumping you. The best thing to do on a wet day is to drink coffee in the kitchen like I did once. Grown up people had better dance the sailors hornpipe or sew. Gentlemen had better warm thear feet and read.'

Their education was not only in the schoolroom. They were taught to be concerned about the poor and to contribute with pocket money and practical gifts to the needy. They must also remember the sick and the dead in their prayers. Emma once brought home a seven-year-old girl whose mother was very ill and whose father, a local shopkeeper, could not look after her. She was known as Winkle, and Emma and her daughters took it in turns to teach her to read and write. She took a great liking to Willie, whom she called Father Ashford, and she always remembered with pleasure the time she spent at Southdown House.

10 VISITORS TO SOUTHDOWN HOUSE

Another popular visitor was Vera's godfather and cousin, Algy Petre. He was one of the seven sons of Sir George Petre who was in the Diplomatic Service, in which Algy also served. References to him in letters show him to have been exceptionally kind. 'We had a school feast yesterday,' wrote Vera in a letter to Julia, 'We had such fun and Algy was father Christmas, and the children made such a noise at him.' He came so often to Lewes that a table napkin ring with his name on it was kept for his use. He was an ideal guest, ready to sing or join in dancing after dinner in the drawing room, to walk on the Downs with the dogs or to sit talking to Willie in the library. But in 1891 his work took him out of Europe. 'I was very sorry to say goodbye,' he wrote to Vera from on board ship, 'But I hope to live to see you all again and to hear that you have been very good and industrious during my absence.' He was on his way to take up the post of translator to the legation at Rio de Janeiro, and when he returned on leave to England two years later he brought with him a pair of marmosets which Emma cared for in the heated greenhouse, and some humming birds which he gave to Lily.

He took a keen interest in Vera's drawing and gave her a course of lessons as a birthday present, promising that on his next visit home he would take her to the South Kensington Museum and, later on, 'When you are more grown up and I am getting wrinkled we may go to Italy and see the treasures of Rome and Florence.' This, however, never took place, for, in 1895, when he was on the point of leaving Brazil to take up an appointment in Madrid, he died from a violent attack of yellow fever. His photograph shows him to have been good looking, with the deep-set eyes of his family, and his death was the first sadness in the lives of the Ashford children.

Algy's brothers used to stay in Lewes, too, usually with their parents. The eldest, George-Ernest, was an eccentric young man with staring eyes, who on one occasion sat next to Daisy at lunch and kept repeating to her in a loud voice, 'My father and I don't get on at all well,' until Sir George was forced to rebuke him, whereupon George-Ernest looked at Daisy as if to say, 'I told you so.' Later in life he developed a dislike of coinage and would only keep £1 notes in his pocket. It was a man-servant's duty to follow him about London and pick up the small change that he refused to accept. Another brother used to carry a hurdy-gurdy about with him and would ask permission to get down from the dinner table so that he could play it.

One can imagine Emma and Willie keeping a sharp eye on the children when such people stayed and imagine, too, the enjoyment of the girls when they could discuss it all later.

Willie was a hospitable man and Emma loved company, so there was a stream of guests during the summer, friends and relations whose names ring strangely in modern ears: Mr Hyde Parker who used to ride down from Petersham on his bicycle attired in knickerbockers and who replied always to offers of biscuits or cakes with the words, 'Thanks, think I will'; Talbot 'Espinasse and Galfridus Crawfurd, both cousins; Alphonsus Guibara and Urquhart Forbes. The latter was nicknamed Turkey by the children who found his name too difficult, and it was taken up by the rest of the family. Turkey had been a fellow oarsman of Willie's on a voyage up the Thames as far as Oxford in 1872, and they had a common interest in the old Roman roads and the waterways of England which led to the joint authorship of *Our Waterways* in 1910.

In Lewes itself they found themselves neighbours of the Robsons, one of whom, Harriet, had married Coventry Patmore as his third wife. Harriet's sisters, Lucy, Lizzie and Charlotte, became great friends of all the Ashfords. Patmore was an old man by then and his health was failing, but he was good company nevertheless and while he rested on a sofa Emma used to read aloud to him; her brisk way of doing so amused him, and her total lack of aesthetic ardour. He, like Willie, was a Tertiary of the Franciscan Order and it is possible that they met at annual retreats at Roehampton.

Agy H E Petre
may 1894.

W. & D. DOWNEY
PHOTOGRAPHERS
57 & 61 EBURY STREET,
LONDON. S.W.

Left: Algy Petre, Vera's Godfather

'The Thirsty Oarsmen' – Willie, Urquhart Forbes ('Turkey'), in the unpressed clothes of the period. Taken in 1872, when they rowed from Walton to Oxford. *Below:* 'Cottage at Nuneham', one of the photographs from Willie's record of their leisurely row downstream.

11 FRIENDS AND ACTING

In the course of their walks round Lewes the Ashford children were intrigued by two girls of their own age whom they noticed one day swinging on a garden gate. The curiosity was mutual, though silent, the presence of the governess ensuring that they should not converse with anyone who was not known to their parents. They continued for some weeks to pass each other in the town, exchanging looks but not words, until the necessary introduction took place, which was the beginning of a lifelong friendship. Nell Ballard was Daisy's particular friend and her sister, Violet, was Angie's. Violet also kept rabbits and many were the arguments they had over the proper method of caring for them. Eventually Angie wrote a handbook which, to Violet's annoyance, was dedicated to her with the subtitle 'Hints to Beginners' on the title page. Mrs Ballard was a nervous but agreeable woman, easily swayed by her daughters, and only too happy at the new acquaintance, and Mr Ballard was one of those figures whose presence was felt in the home but rarely outside it. The friendship between the girls progressed so well that eventually it was decided that they should do their lessons together.

Though devoted to their parents, especially to their father, Daisy, Vera and Angie had a great desire to go to school. It seemed such an exciting world, filled with new friends, intriguing surroundings and amusing rules. They were very interested in the activities of the local school and attended any prize-givings or outings that they were allowed to, and they knew the names of the children and the sort of homes they came from.

Now, instead of lessons at Southdown House with their own governess, they went every day to Miss Mable Smythe, the daughter of a Lewes doctor, and a very capable teacher. There, with the addition of the rector's daughter and, of course, the two little Ballards, they numbered six, and leaving their own house every morning laden with books and pencil cases, they could pretend that they were attending a real school.

Soon the idea came to them that, with their greater numbers, they could produce a play of their own, and they turned to Emma for advice. She did not fail them. They decided on *Cinderella* and the parts, five in number, were allotted between the Ballards and the Ashfords (the rector's daughter not taking part). Nell and Daisy played Proud Sisters nos. I and II; Vera, Prince Putapenni Intheslot; and Angie, with her flaxen hair, Cinderella. Violet, who was extremely shy, played the Fairy God-mother. When not engaged in their roles they sang offstage, often while changing for the next scene. There are marginal notes by Emma, 'Nell & Daisy rush off to change' or 'Cinderella keeps on blue stockings'.

Emma wrote *Cinderella* in verse, the metre changing from scene to scene, and the songs were set to a variety of music hall and traditional airs. Lewes church hall was lent to them on condition that, after the performance for the Catholic school children, they should give another the following night for the children of the Church of England school. Emma and Lily made the costumes and, with the assistance of a carpenter, arranged the scenery, and Emma insisted on the production being as professional as possible. Family and friends, as well as the school children, filled the chairs in the auditorium and the sale of the programmes and tickets, designed by Vera, was witnessed by the cast through a crack in the curtains.

The success of *Cinderella* inspired Daisy herself to write a play, performed this time in the schoolroom at Southdown House. A stage was erected, and curtains and scenery arranged again by Emma. Although the manuscript was lost, several choice pieces of dialogue were remembered and handed down to posterity. It was entitled *A Woman's Crime*, Angie playing the heroine, stabbed to death by Vera. The butler informs the lady of the house that her daughter is lying dead upstairs; 'I will go to her at once,' she announces. 'Oh, no, madam,' the butler says repressively, 'I will bring the body down.' The murderess is eventually unmasked and driven from the house with the words, 'Go, guilty woman, from this house, bearing upon your soul and character the blot of a woman's crime.'

This thriller was witnessed by Ernest and two actor friends who were obliged to stuff handkerchiefs in their mouths to stifle their laughter.

Commenced June 14 1896.

A. Book
ON RABBITS
& Guinea Pigs.

By ANGELA ASHFORD.

Dedicated to .VIOLET.BALLARD

Hints to Beginners.

Above: The title page of Angie's work on rabbit care

Left: Programme for *Cinderella*, designed by Vera

12 EDUCATION AND DEVELOPMENT

Compared to modern children the Ashford sisters were quite ignorant of the world. They lived a sheltered life and their childhood lingered on into what is now considered a separate stage of development, adolescence. They knew nothing about the sexual side of love, only the romantic. Lily had thrilled them with the account of an admirer holding her hand, kissing her and then saying, 'I wish this little hand were mine,' but it was not until many years later that they discovered poor Lily had thought the kiss was enough to make her pregnant, and that she had passed many agonising days as a result. Emma never informed any of her five daughters of the 'facts of life', a rather uncharacteristic omission from such a forthright person. So they grew up ignorant and innocent in this respect.

Again, by modern standards their education was very inadequate. Subjects that are now part of the standard school curriculum − geography, all branches of mathematics and the sciences, economics and politics − they either missed altogether or learned out of school hours. And yet Willie could write to Vera in 1899, when she was sixteen and away at school for the first time, 'The Cabinet Council yesterday decided to send an ultimatum demanding a complete concession of "suzerainty", which I fancy Kruger could not grant now if he would, for the younger generation of Boers are much more hot headed and determined than they were 17 years ago, and are even now said to be threatening our force on the Natal frontier where we have barely 3,000 men.' Although so young, Vera was expected to understand and comment on her father's news.

When they were young they read children's stories, some, like Maria Edgeworth's, pitilessly moral, but mostly the delightful stories of their own time, *Penelope and the Others*, *Happy Go Lucky*, *Vice Versa*, and also, of course, Dickens. Later they were encouraged to read from the variety of books in Willie's library. Vera's interest in history and military matters he carefully nurtured, and when they were old enough they were given Thackeray, the Brontës and Jane Austen (referred to by Julia as 'Miss Austen'). He would then want to know what they thought of them, gravely comparing their opinions with his own and expecting them to defend theirs. Poetry they learned from their governess, as well as from their parents, and later in life could still recite much of Tennyson, Browning, Wordsworth, Coleridge and Scott.

I think it was to Willie that all three owed their critical sense. His standards were high, and on the subject of music he wrote to Vera in March 1900, 'You will, I think, find that a knowledge of theory helps you very much to enjoy and appreciate good music, and you will be able, after a bit, to "analyse" a piece – that is, to pick it to pieces and notice the various phrases by which the composer develops his ideas, as also the changes of key, harmony, etc.' But, even to please her father, Vera could not pretend to his love of music, and it was left to Angie to explore it with him.

They grew up, educated largely and, in a sense, unconsciously by their parents, their father, scholarly and pious, having the greater influence on them, and their mother providing, perhaps, the vital spark that started Daisy writing.

It is interesting to note the distribution of talents and characteristics among the three sisters as they grew older. They could all, when pressed, write verses for the paper games they used to play, but Angie was the only one who could dash off the same sort of absurd and clever jingles that Emma did so well. They all wrote clear English and exchanged long and amusing letters with each other throughout their lives.

Vera, as has been said, became an artist like her grandfather, the amiable William Ker Ashford; she was also the greatest reader (largely because she suffered from insomnia); and she was the most intellectually akin to Julia.

They all learned to play the piano and sing, but Angie was the only one to inherit Willie's great love of music.

Vera was an excellent nurse like her mother, and possessed that inner courage and strength that made her the obvious choice to help in emergencies of every kind.

All three were tremendous talkers and they used often to sit up through the night, sustained by cups of tea. Their voices were pleasantly low-pitched and they read aloud beautifully.

Angie, her mother's favourite, had Willie's reserve and his quiet sense of humour. Her shyness never affected her keen observation and she was, I think, the best mimic from a family of mimics. In character she very much resembled Julia. And Vera, her father's favourite, most resembled Emma in character; and she copied Emma's use of the short 'a' in words like grass and castle (Emma's mother came from Ayrshire), while Daisy and Angie used the long 'a'. She had a strong temper, not easily roused, and a passionate loyalty to her father.

Daisy herself was the one member of the family with whom it was impossible to quarrel, and she was the general favourite, quite unresentful of her sisters' position. But, indeed, both parents were exceptionally loving and it would have been hard for her to feel neglected. She had the peace-maker's qualities of understanding and sympathy and a total absence of self-regard.

13 DAISY'S AND ANGIE'S STORIES

In 1892, when she was eleven years old, Daisy wrote *The True History of Leslie Woodcock*, a birthday present for her mother. As in *The Young Visiters* her command of English is astonishing and she wickedly shuts the door in the reader's face when his curiosity is at its height and switches to the doings of another character which soon become as absorbing as those of the first. Letters and conversation flow and descriptions of clothes and meals, but the London of this story is not the high society of *The Young Visiters*. Here are narrow streets and cheap lodging houses into which the hero, Leslie, takes Sylvia when they elope, although he had started out with '£40 in ready gold'. Her characters are endearingly human. Leslie has not the courage to tell old Nan how disgusting is the room she has let to them or that he had to sit up all night;

and Sylvia, once married, removes her gloves in the restaurant so that people can see her new wedding ring. Her uncle, whose disapproval of the marriage was the reason for the elopement, becomes desperately ill, and they return home. It is a simple story, but like all Daisy's writings, utterly absorbing and amusing.

In the same year Angie wrote *The Jealous Governes*. While Daisy concentrated on love and marriage, eight-year-old Angie broached the subject of birth, describing the doctor arriving with the baby in a cardboard box tied up with string. She had obviously heard that mothers are in bed on these occasions so she makes Mrs Hose receive the doctor in her bedroom. All her life Angie had a love of babies and an understanding of children; here she tells the story of a baby boy kidnapped by his governess, and the happy ending is that the boy, now twenty, is re-united with his father. It is funny and touching, and Angie has, like Daisy, a very observant eye.

Vera's only story, which was of a pious nature and called *Little Mary and the Angle*, must have been written about this time, but is unfortunately lost. Perhaps it was put away with Angie's next story, *Treacherous Mr Campbell*, for that also is missing.

A letter written by Daisy in 1893, one of the very few dated letters, is addressed to her father, who was staying with Julia in Petersham. The influence of the governess is obvious in the copper-plate handwriting and in the lay-out.

My Angel lamb love Pops,

I hope you arrived quite safely, & also that you found Auntie quite well.

The little Ballards came to tea on Saturday, I mean only Nellie came, we enjoyed ourselves very much & we played rounders after tea. Fr McAuliffe read the pastoral at second Mass, & he kept shutting his eyes & putting his hand on his chest.

I dressed all my dolls in their Sunday clothes yesterday, & I am going to trim Charley a new hat for next time & also May, because Gereldine and Ethel have got new ones. I went to Sunday school yesterday, & also to Vespers.

Miss Prenleloup [the French governess] had a lovely hat on yesterday, it was very thin white straw, trimmed with white silk bows & forgetme-nots, she also had on an all white dress, she looked so innocent, you would have liked to see her.

I am writing to Auntie today. Yesterday was Miss Prenleloup's birth-day. It is very hot today, in the bottom greenhouse it is simply awful. They are cutting the grass in Colenal Cumberlidge's field. There are heaps of dog daisies in the tennis lawn. I have no more news to tell you so
with best love & kisses
I am
Every your loving daughter
Daisy

At twelve she was still playing with dolls, but surely that particular stage of her imaginative life was drawing to its close.

She was engaged that year on *Where Love Lies Deepest* (the titles of her stories are always memorable), a story, from the hero's point of view, of unrequited love. Here is a great step forward towards maturity, and the opening description of the moonlit night is excellent. The heroine, Beatrice, refuses to marry without love – 'I almost love you, Lawrence,' she says, 'But I cannot marry you,' and she sticks to her word in spite of her own poverty and his wealth. For the first time morality comes into her work, and mature feeling. Nor is there a conventional happy ending; Lawrence dies, though not before Beatrice has declared her love for him at last in a passionate deathbed scene.

Her next and final story was *The Hangman's Daughter*, and she put more effort into this than into any of her others. Barrie remarked of *The Young Visiters* that it needed no effort 'for that face to knock off a masterpiece', and I think the only effort required for her earlier stories was that of sitting down and using her pencil – the words poured in marvellous profusion as, from her child's view, she observed the world. But now she is no longer a child her view has shifted, although her imagination is as rich. The new story took her about a year to write and the self-discipline necessary for such a lengthy process for a fourteen-year-old girl is quite admirable. No wonder she was proud of it. It is, of course, extremely funny, particularly when she is most serious. The heroine, Helen, was based on Daisy's great friend, Nell Ballard, who was as excited as Daisy could have wished to be put in a book.

Her plot is ingenious: the heroine and her best friend spend the greater part of the story engaged to the two villains and the heroes only make their appearance towards the end. Her characters are full-blooded people who fly into rages, faint, sing and eat even more heartily than those in her previous stories. And her style is more mature, so that the unintentionally comic parts are the funnier, coming as they do between vivid descriptions or touching passages that a writer three times her age would feel a glow of satisfaction at having written.

With the completion of *The Hangman's Daughter* Daisy Ashford's work as child author came to an end, as though her childhood had been packed away with her last manuscript, and she took her first unsteady steps into that adult world of which she had known so little but about which she had written to such effect. There was never any suggestion that her stories might be sent to a publisher, then or later; they were simply considered necessary stepping stones to the real books she would write when she was grown up.

Why did she stop writing? She herself said that the ambition to be a writer left her after her school days, and she put this down (in a radio interview years later) to laziness. Or did she suspect that her talent would not survive in the adult world? Or did she recognise her lack of ruthlessness, or jib at the solitude necessary to a writer? We cannot know.

14 SCHOOL AND AFTER

The daily lessons with Mabel Smythe continued but Emma was not satisfied with her daughters' progress. She considered that they were growing up 'wild and ignorant' and she cast around for a remedy. In the village of Haywards Heath about twelve miles away a convent had been founded and a school started in the previous decade, and it was decided that the girls should go there. The Priory was an enclosed order, which meant that the nuns remained always within the convent walls, and only the pupils and lay staff appeared beyond them from time to time. There was a portress whose job it was to inspect visitors through a small window before admitting them, and her face, with the black veil pulled forward to conceal as much of it as possible, was all that the visitor saw of her. *Bona fides* having been established, she manipulated the lock by remote control from her cubby hole, and when the heavy door had swung open her disembodied voice directed the visitor to turn left along the passage and then right into the parlour. This was an austere and highly polished room with a grill dividing it in two. Any nun who was called to the parlour pulled her veil down over her forehead before entering through a door on the other side of the grill. To a non-Catholic it could be quite an ordeal. The enclosure had so alarmed the villagers of Haywards Heath when the nuns first settled there that, to allay their fears, permission was obtained from the bishop to open the grounds to them for a day, and they wandered about the school and gardens finding nothing out of the ordinary except the medieval habits of the nuns, who welcomed them all in a friendly way.

Daisy was seventeen when she donned a school uniform for the first time and was taken by train to Haywards Heath, and her sisters were left disconsolately at home; for Vera was not to go to the Priory until the following year. In fact Daisy left before Vera started, each of them enjoying only a year of school life. Angie was the only one to stay longer, from 1900 to 1902. Coming so late to school they found the rules more of an interesting novelty than a burden and they entered into the life of the place with ease. They made friends, missed their father, who used to ride over on his bicycle to see them whenever possible, and passed the examinations required of them. Daisy, on receiving a letter from Willie saying that he would be passing through Haywards Heath on a certain train sent off a telegram to him reading, 'Please stick bird's head out of window Haywards Heath' (they were going through a phase of calling

Music Rooms, Priory Haywards Heath.

Priory of Our Lady of Good Counsel
4 - Old House and entrance to Hall.

Above left: Mabel Smythe's class, 1898. *Standing:* Vera a 16, Katie Jickling, Violet Ballard. *Sitting:* Daisy aged Angie, 14, and Nell Ballard.

Above & left: The Priory, Haywards Heath in 1900

him 'bird'), and she managed to slip down to the station in time to see Willie waving to her as the train sped through the station.

At eighteen Daisy was back at home with no more lessons to do, and finding that glorious grown-up life to which she had looked forward so much really rather dull. Emma, whose own life had been so eventful, who had hunted, gone to balls and flirted so happily, seems to have made no effort to launch her attractive daughters in the world. It was Ettie and Lily all over again. Daisy had a good figure and complexion, her abundant hair was wavy and light brown and she had great charm. Vera's hair, like Emma's, was long and dark, her skin paler than Daisy's and her figure slimmer. Angie retained her flaxen hair and had the very fair skin that goes with it. She was not such a great walker as her sisters and was very shy. Daisy and Vera thought nothing of tramping ten or fifteen miles, and once did a twenty mile walk, to be regaled with whisky and hot water by Willie on their return home.

Owing to Emma's extravagant ways Willie's capital was by now considerably reduced. Except for some land in Ireland inherited from Colonel 'Espinasse, he owned no property, and his income came largely from investments. It is an extraordinary fact that after leaving the War Office he never worked for his living, but lived resignedly on a steadily diminishing income. There was no thought of asking fashionable cousins to 'bring out' the Ashford girls, or even sending them on a round of visits such as Julia had enjoyed as a girl. It is also probable that Willie considered the fashionable world of 1900 decidedly vulgar. The writer remembers Vera speaking of the 'Marlborough House Set' with great disapproval. So the social life of the sisters was confined to concert- and theatre-going in Brighton, cycling with friends, picnics and tea parties, tame stuff after the entertainments Daisy had invented in her stories.

In 1904 they moved to Bexhill and Vera left home for London where she enrolled at the Slade and had a studio of her own. Her accounts of student parties and dances became more than Daisy could bear and she, too, went to London to do a secretarial course; the sisters lived together on and off until the Great War, Vera painting and designing and Daisy working as a secretary.

Opposite: Willie in the garden at Bexhill; favourite photograph

Above left: Daisy at 18. Grown up at last

Above right: A Slade picnic about 1906.
Vera standing at the back

Right: Emma in widow's weeds

Overleaf: Daisy in fancy dress by Vera

Inset: Baa by F. K. Mayer, a fellow student of Vera's

John Hicks's

14 DEVONSHIRE ROAD
BEXHILL-ON-SEA

In 1905 Julia died at Byam Cottage at the age of seventy-one. She left her modest possessions to her brother, and there were bequests of five guineas each to the Petersham Coal Club, the Aged Poor Society, the Providence Row Refuge and a dozen other charities. With her death the Ashford connection with Petersham ended.

Willie survived Julia by seven years, dying in 1912 in his seventy-sixth year. He was mourned by his children as tenderly as they had loved him during his lifetime, and his goodness was spoken of by them to the grandchildren that he never lived to know.

The following year Angie, who had lived at home with her parents after leaving school, was married, and Emma was left with only the moody Lily for company. But since the arthritis from which she had suffered for years was becoming worse, Daisy and Vera decided to give up their studio in London to come home and help to look after and amuse her. Her adored Angie did not live far away and was able to visit her often and bring her baby daughter with her, the only one of Willie's grandchildren Emma was to see.

In 1917, with her daughters round her, Emma died. She was buried next to Willie in the Catholic cemetery at Bexhill, and her children began the ritual dismantling of their home.

15 THE PUBLICATION OF 'THE YOUNG VISITERS'

At the time of her mother's death Daisy was thirty-five, still an attractive woman with the dark, very bright eyes that we see in early photographs. To her expression now was added amusement for, like Emma, she had the happy knack of extracting enjoyment from even the most trivial events, although, unlike Emma, she was shy. She had done what war work she could in Bexhill but after Emma's death and the closing of the house the sisters separated, Daisy to run a canteen in Dover and Vera to drive lorries in London and Glasgow.

It was while they were sorting through Emma's papers that they came upon a box, familiar to most mothers, where their childhood relics had been carefully preserved – first efforts at letter writing and drawing, Vera's 'last will and testimony', and exercise books containing Daisy's and Angie's stories. These last Daisy rescued from being put into store and they were read amid gales of laughter. What Daisy had written in such deadly earnest, those telling phrases and words that she had been so proud of, now shouted joyfully at her across the intervening years. She wrote typically of herself, 'I can never feel all the nice things that have been said about *The Young Visiters* are really due to me at all, but to a Daisy Ashford of so long ago that she seems almost another person.' *The Young Visiters* was the story they all liked best and Mr Salteena and his 'idears' came to be quoted in their letters to each other.

The following year it happened that a friend of Daisy's, Margaret Mackenzie, had a bad attack of 'flu and Daisy, hoping to cheer her out of the depression that followed her illness, gave her *The Young Visiters* to read. It worked like a charm, and so funny did Margaret find it that she asked Daisy to make a copy for her. Daisy had by this time left her canteen in Dover to work in the Foreign Office and she gave Margaret the copy of her book before setting off for Switzerland where she was to take up a post at the British Legation in Berne.

Margaret Mackenzie was a distinguished-looking woman, one of a large Catholic family, who had known the Ashfords all their lives. She had been on the stage, she wrote poetry, reviewed books, was a founder of the Catholic Stage Guild and knew a great many people in the theatre and the literary world.

In the course of a weekend in the country Margaret produced *The Young Visiters* after dinner and read a chapter aloud to the company. Everyone was enchanted and amused, and none more so than Mr Frank Swinnerton, who was among the guests, and who asked if he might borrow the book when he went to bed that night. He was working at the time for Chatto & Windus as reader and editor, and when he and Margaret met at breakfast next morning he talked to her of the possibility of publishing it. Margaret was delighted and cabled to Daisy for permission, and Daisy, surprised that anything she had written might be thought worth putting into print, gave her consent. Shortly afterwards Frank Swinnerton was able to lay the original manuscript before the publishers.

There was no doubt that the book should be published, and the only question was how it should be presented. Although a complete novel it was very short, and the fact that the author was only nine years old when she wrote it had to be explained.

Swinnerton sent a copy to J. M. Barrie who was then at the height of his fame and reputation as an authority on the working of children's imagination. While it was in his hands Swinnerton wrote to Margaret Mackenzie, 'The Young Visiters is a work of genius and I am enchanted with it . . . We should really like very much to publish the work prefaced by some sort of assurance that it is the authentic work of a young person.' The assurance, he hoped, would be provided by Barrie in the form of a preface and he was delighted to receive Barrie's whole-hearted approval of the book in a letter dated 7th February 1919:

Dear Mr Swinnerton,

There is no doubt that 'The Young Visiters' (which perhaps ought to be called 'The Pot of Ruge') is a scrumptious affair and fit to make the right people jump for joy. I find myself turning back to it for advice, instruction and amusement, and mourning the melancholy case of an authoress who could do this when she was nine and is now occupied in putting up her hair or something of the kind. I have a feeling that at some period of the MS.'s history there has been a slight meddling with it by older hands. 'Then he sat down and eat the egg that Ethel had so kindly laid for him', and a few other touches seem suspicious to me. But in any case the thing as a whole is too masterly to have come from any brain but a child's.

I don't know how it would come out as a book. That seems to me to weight it. The choicest thing would be to print it privately for the delectation of what you and I might consider the crowned heads. Another plan, to make a magazine article of it, not printing all but most with a running commentary. I'd be ready to do this for, say, Scribners (the payment of course to be the lady's) tho' I think I'd be the wrong man

– having dealt a bit in children I might be suspect. I cant see why you dont do it yourself. Probably also you prefer the book idea. In any case, loud applause to you for having shown it to me.

Yours sincerely

J. M. Barrie

Advice from Barrie was not to be ignored but Swinnerton felt that although the 'crowned heads' would undoubtedly appreciate *The Young Visiters* to the full, there was really a much wider audience for such a book, and that to reach it a cheap edition was essential. The necessity of an introduction remained and Swinnerton was sure he could persuade Barrie to write it. In his book, *The Georgian Literary Scene*, he describes his meeting with the great man at his flat in Adelphi Terrace. 'Our conversation,' he writes, 'was marked by slowness and hesitation upon his side, and promptness on my own.' Barrie was a sick man at the time and no match for the determined Swinnerton, and after suggesting a number of people, each one of whom would, he said, write an excellent preface and each one of whom was rejected by Swinnerton, a great silence fell. The silence worked visibly on Barrie and at length he said, 'I see I've got to write this preface.'

Before embarking on it, however, he wanted to see the original manuscript and to know what sort of childhood Daisy had enjoyed and, above all, what had started her writing. The correspondence was carried on through Swinnerton and Daisy said of her writing, 'I very occasionally asked for a word to describe something and wrote whatever they suggested in all seriousness . . . My father always refused to give me even a word saying it was my story and not his, but my mother and grown-up step-sisters would always come to the rescue . . . We saw more of grown-up people than other children, and speaking for myself they always interested me far more.'

Daisy had returned to England in February to be plunged into incessant activity and to find her name already known to the literary world. She continued her secretarial work in an office off Victoria Street, and her spare time was taken up with correspondence and the numerous con-

98

Above Left: Daisy in 1919, after the publication of
The Young Visiters

Above: Daisy, 1919

Left: Margaret Mackenzie

sultations and decisions required by the publishers. She found Swinnerton enthusiastic and helpful with information and advice, and a rapport was established at once between them.

Margaret Mackenzie, unwilling to relinquish her role as discoverer of the child prodigy, continued to act as go-between on the subject of terms, but after the signing of the agreement at the end of February 1919, she withdrew, and Daisy herself conducted all the correspondence. It is fair to say that she was probably only too glad of Margaret's advice and help, and Margaret was certainly determined that Daisy should make the most of her success. She organised tea and dinner parties to enable her to meet her literary friends.

With a possible American market in view, Swinnerton advised Daisy to send a copy of the book to George H. Doran, his publisher in New York, mentioning his name, and some weeks later came the cable, 'Accept Young Visiters, forwarding contract. Mail two copies for copyright. Doran.'

Daisy's leisure hours now became much more hectic than her office work, and the nearer the date of publication the busier she was, correcting proofs and attending meetings. The dust cover by Norman Wilkinson appealed strongly to her; she felt that he had drawn Mr Salteena to the life and particularly liked the thin strand of hair sticking out at the back of his head.*

'I never thought in my life,' wrote Daisy to Swinnerton in May, 'I should experience such a thrill as getting a book published. It really does quite stagger me. I never thought even when I got Miss Mackenzie's wire in Switzerland, anything more than it would be exciting to see a work of my own in print and how thrilled my mother and father would have been if they were alive.'

Two days before publication, which was to be 22nd May, Swinnerton wrote to her, 'I think you will be glad to know that already, before publication, we are reprinting *The Young Visiters*. This is excellent. The

---

* There were no illustrations. The first illustrated edition of *The Young Visiters* was published in 1949 with pictures by Heather Corlass. A new edition, illustrated by Posy Simmonds, was published in 1984.

tainable, through the medical omcer...
health of the patient's district, at certain
medical institutions in London.

NOVEL BY GIRL OF 9.

SIR JAMES BARRIE CALLS IT "SCRUMPTIOUS."

A 10,000 words novel by a gir
be published next month by Mess
and Windus. Sir James Barri
written an introduction to the
E. V. Lucas, and others desc
" scream."

The authoress is Miss Da
the daughter of a War Offic
The Weekly Dispatch. She
more than 9 now, but has
called " The Young Visiter
book in which she origina
will be published just as
including all its childish
ing, grammar and the
obvious one in the title.

The novel was discove
Swinnerton, reader to W
Windus. A friend wh
says, " enjoyed it so t
got permission to pass
some persuasion the au
lish it, though with :
siasm.

" " The Young Vis
troduction, and I
Barrie was the one
has sent his introd
says: " The Young
tious affair, and fit
people jump with i

THE FIRST PAGE.

The sub-title of
is " Mr. Salteen
of the manuscri
was an elderly r
asking people t
quite a young i
named Ethel
has dark, she
whiskers wh
twisty. He
This " eld
in the story
to pay anot
who is no
arrive the
culine frie
each oth
parts for
appears,
ment an
more a
Soon
Mounti
they p
and p
highe
of th
land
trea
hur

THE 400,000 COPIES BOOK.

HOW I FOUND IT.

By FRANK SWINNERTON,

The Well-known Novelist who acts as Reader to Messrs. Chatto and Windus, the Publishers of "The Young Visiters."

It must be, I should think, one of the most delightful sensations in the world to wake up one morning and find oneself famous. It must be like a miracle. That is what happened this

MISS DAISY ASHFORD.

year to Daisy Ashford when her now world-famous novel, "The Young Visiters," was published.

It is a romance of publishing without parallel. When Daisy Ashford was a little girl she and her sisters lived in the lovely town of Lewes, and spent a great deal of time on the Downs with their mother, a charming, high-spirited woman, who defied the ordinary laws of the school-room and whisked the children off for unexpected picnics in a way to make one hold one's breath in envy.

No wonder the children were happy, with such a mother and in such surroundings! But they had a time of very great freedom, and this trained their wits as nothing else could have done. Constant fresh air, the society of those older than themselves—and three little women grew up both wise and care-free.

Each year, on the anniversary of their parents' marriage, they drew wonderful pictures and wrote wonderful poems commemorating some incident in the courtship and marriage of father and mother—the proposal, a picnic, the wedding, and so on. They dressed up and performed little plays. They read voraciously. And they wrote little novels. Several of these ...
read with delight by
composition.

THE £1 BABY

One, by or

---

ght: Newspaper accounts of the
blication of *The Young Visiters*

ow: the cover of the first edition of
e Young Visiters drawn by Norman
lkinson

THE YOUNG
VISITERS
BY
DAISY ASHFORD

WITH A PREFACE BY
J. M. BARRIE

first impression consists of 1,500 copies. It is not all sold but it will be. One bookseller who had ordered seven copies, has increased his order, after reading the book, to fifty.'

The demand for *The Young Visiters* was immediate and enormous and the bookshops were selling it as fast as supplies could be delivered. A week later Swinnerton was able to tell Daisy that every copy of the second impression had been ordered by booksellers before it was printed, as well as half the third impression, and that a fourth had just been ordered.

Reviews in the press were almost unanimous in their praise: 'This little book,' wrote the critic in the *Daily Telegraph*, 'has been much proclaimed in advance and great expectations have been aroused for it, but the thing itself is a thousand times better than any "puff" preliminary.' A long, appreciative article appeared in the *Manchester Guardian*, 'There is nothing fanciful or tender in it . . . It is the work of an intensely dogged and practical mind, with an amazing vocabulary and a keen observation . . . Her sophistication,' he added, 'is overpowering at times.'

It was difficult to write about the book without quoting extensively from it, as Barrie in his preface discovered. There was no yardstick by which to judge it. The *Daily News* doubted whether it could be classed as fiction at all; 'It is more like satire,' was the conclusion. 'The public owe Miss Daisy Ashford a debt of gratitude,' the article goes on, 'for the privilege of being allowed for once to know something of how the world looks to a child of nine, even if the child be a somewhat sophisticated girl.'

The *Daily Mail* was more guarded, calling *The Young Visiters* 'a work of precocity not of genius,' and the *Times Literary Supplement* was patronising: 'Other people, too,' the critic remarked, after reporting Barrie's enjoyment of the book, 'may enjoy a glance at it, for the quaintness, naïveté and deficient punctuation of children's original composition are always amusing.'

The publication of *The Young Visiters* created the sort of stir that publishers dream about, and, as Swinnerton himself wrote, 'It was . . . the greatest success enjoyed in a single season by any book published by Chatto & Windus.' Photographs of Daisy began to appear in the press and interviews, which she found intensely disagreeable, were foisted on her. She soon refused to meet the press at all, a fact that made her even more appealing to the keen reporter. Vera, on ordering something from a shop in London, was asked if she was any relation of *the* Daisy Ashford, and on admitting the fact, she was surrounded by excited assistants who abandoned their customers in order to talk to the sister of such a celebrity.

Daisy relished every moment of her success. She rode on the crest of the wave but she never lost her head, or looked on her rocketing fame as anything more than a glorious party.

Very soon, as Barrie had foreseen, voices were raised suggesting that *The Young Visiters* was an elaborate hoax played upon the public by Barrie himself. It was too clever, too neatly finished off to be the work of a child. Winston Churchill maintained this point of view and sought to prove it by careful quotation from the book. Swinnerton was buttonholed in the street by a woman journalist who asked simply, 'Did HE or did SHE?' Daisy's stepbrother, Baa, overheard an argument on the subject at a nearby table in a restaurant where he was dining and could not resist joining in the conversation in support of his sister.

A few months later poor Barrie told Charles Scribner, the American publisher, that there was 'no foundation for any report . . . that I had anything whatever to do with *The Young Visiters* beyond writing the preface. It is printed word for word as originally shown me. I think I say this in preface, and I rather resent people's not accepting my word. The whole affair has been something of a trial for me,' he added plaintively, 'as hordes of parents here keep sending me their children's works, and now they are doing it from America. I have to employ a secretary.'

Daisy, too, was the recipient of the manuscript of a book written by a friend of hers at the age of thirteen, and, after reading it dutifully, she sent it on, with apologies, to Chatto & Windus.

It was two weeks after publication before a meeting between Barrie and Daisy took place; he invited her to tea. The interview, about which she was very nervous, passed off better than she had expected, although the long silences to which Barrie was prone had a 'petrifying effect' on her. In July she went again, this time accompanied by Margaret, and she described it to Swinnerton: 'The visit was much more of a success than when I went alone. He was much more talkative and friendly.' The self-assurance of Margaret had obviously allayed the shyness of the other two and enabled them to converse with comparative ease. Barrie told them he had received a cable from America asking for dramatic rights for 'Mr Salteena' (his generosity in writing the preface seemed to bring him only the irritation of being regarded as a talent spotter, a hoaxer or a dispenser of rights that he did not possess), and the problems of turning the book into a play were discussed. Daisy wrote, 'He said *he* couldn't do it as he was so busy, but that it could be done, only it would be very difficult.' It was a problem that still teased him when he went off to Scotland soon afterwards. And it was an idea, too, that attracted Margaret Mackenzie and her sister, Siney (who wrote novels under the pen-name of Mrs George Norman). *They* would write the play of *The Young Visiters* themselves. Margaret's early experience on the stage combined with Siney's talent as a writer could not fail to produce a successful dramatisation.

They asked for Daisy's agreement to their scheme, which she readily gave, but before long a letter arrived from Barrie saying that he had had one or two ideas on the subject and thought that, after all, he could turn *The Young Visiters* into a play. Daisy and Vera were staying with Margaret at her house in Rye, and they discussed this proposal from one of the most skilful and successful playwrights of the day. Daisy and Vera waited for Margaret and Siney to withdraw from the scene in favour of Barrie, but they waited in vain. At length Vera called Margaret out of the room and asked her bluntly, 'Do you want to make money for Daisy or for yourselves?' 'Oh, for Daisy, of course,' replied Margaret. 'Then let Barrie write it,' said Vera. They returned to the room, where Margaret and her sister were polite, but refused to withdraw, and Daisy, having given her word, could do no more than write what she described as a very difficult letter to Barrie, telling him that she had already given the option to Margaret. He took the gravest offence and all communication with

Daisy was ended. This story was told to the writer by Vera many years later. It was typical of Daisy's character that in spite of this episode she attended the opening night of the play in 1920, accompanied by the co-authors. It is tantalising to think what sort of play Barrie would have written.

The book continued, meanwhile, to sell at a gratifying rate.* A copy was presented to Queen Mary, it was put into Braille and translated into French. Permission was asked to make Ethel Monticue dolls, and Mr Henry Melville asked to use the story as the scenario for a ballet.

Instances of its therapeutic effect on war casualties still in hospital were passed on to Daisy. She was deeply touched to hear of men who had been sunk in apathy being able to laugh at what she had written. One woman wrote that her gravely wounded husband, who had not so much as smiled for over a year, had been rendered helpless with laughter over *The Young Visiters*.

Chatto & Windus fended off the journalists who wanted to interview Daisy, but occasionally, when Swinnerton felt she really ought to be interviewed, she agreed, though reluctantly.

The laughter that the book provoked was probably the more enjoyable because it came just after four years of war; Germans were still being referred to in the press as 'Huns' and there was unrest at home and abroad as the fruits of victory were argued over. Notices of the book appeared at the same time as announcements of a case of bubonic plague in Liverpool, rabies in London, and the grisly details of the Landru murders in France. Against such a background *The Young Visiters* was pure joy.

In July Daisy was asked to read a chapter of the book at an At Home, and gave an account of that and a further reading on the same day, to Swinnerton. 'The parties were great sport. I felt awfully nervous at the start at Lady Moreton's, for being a distinctly "society" function where the guests literally sat in rows on golden chairs, their laughter was not of

---

* By 1984 sales in the United Kingdom had reached over 270,000, and in the United States they had reached 200,000 by 1975, just short of the quarter of a million required for the book to be classified as a bestseller.

that hilarity that makes you know it's going well. However, they begged for more when I stopped and were so appreciative when they talked that I bucked up and felt far more full of vim when I got to Lord Latham's in the evening. Here it was a great success . . . and we all sat on cushions on the floor and had supper in Lord L.'s bedroom, so you can imagine it was a far more homely gathering and great fun.'

In November 1919, a film company approached her, 'Please chase off the gentleman who wants me to go on the film,' she begged Mr Spalding of Chatto & Windus, 'I'd *very* much rather be shot through the heart and don't a bit mind telling him so.'

An invitation to do a lecture tour of America the following year was certainly tempting, but in the same month Daisy became engaged to be married and she turned the offer down. She had continued her secretarial job all through these busy months, fitting the life of a newly successful author into her lunch hours, the evenings and weekends, but, on becoming engaged, she resigned.

In January 1920, a few weeks before the first performance of *The Young Visiters* at Ramsgate, she stepped down with some relief from the crest of the wave she had been riding and married James Devlin. As far as she was concerned it had been a lovely party.

16 THE AUTHOR IN RETIREMENT

After their marriage Daisy and James Devlin settled in Norfolk. True to the Ashford tendency to marry late, Daisy was thirty-nine when her first child, Margie, was born. Her second daughter, Clare, was born in 1923, and then came two boys, the youngest of whom was born in 1926 when Daisy was forty-five.

Vera, too, married in 1920, and inevitably, from this time on, meetings between the three sisters, with their increasing families, became fewer.

In June 1920, Daisy's other stories were published in England and the United States under the title *Daisy Ashford: Her Book*, including at the

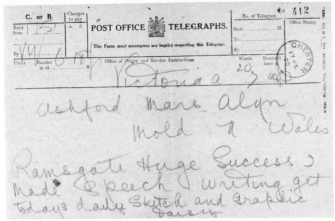

Above: J. M. Barrie by W. T. Monnington, reproduced by permission of the National Portrait Gallery, London

Top: Daisy's telegram to Vera after the first night of the play of *The Young Visiters* at Ramsgate in 1920

Right: Newspaper account of the first night. 1920

'THE YOUNG VISITERS' STAGED.

Well Received by Critical Audience, Book in Hand.

COSTLY CROWN ON VIEW.

From Our Special Correspondent.

RAMSGATE, Monday: Daisy Ashford was a proud woman to-night.

Sitting in a box at the Palace Theatre, Ramsgate, by the side of her young husband, she listened to the first performance of the dramatised version of her book, "The Young Visiters," and watched the audience laugh till it cried.

She and her husband had come over from Rye, where they had been spending their honeymoon.

Audience Who Knew.

A crowded house gave the play a splendid reception.

The audience, nevertheless, was a critical one. Nearly everybody carried a copy of the book, and all were obviously familiar with the text.

No story has suffered less by dramatisation. The whole of the book is faithfully produced by Mrs. George Norman and Miss Margaret Mackenzie.

Daisy Ashford's swift, destructive sentences are worked into dialogue

It was "The Young Visiters" pure and unadulterated. There was no bowdlerisation: even the accidental *double entente* of the childish mind was reproduced.

The Court Scene.

The court scene was the best. The Prince of Wales, with a golden beard and his "small but costly crown" was the centre of a tit-bit of burlesque.

Miss Edyth Goodall as Ethel Monticue struck the right atmosphere and retained it. Mr. Ben Field made an excellently apprehensive Mr. Salteena, while Mr. Harold Anstruthers (Bernard Clark), "with his nice long legs," and his languid air, and Mr. John Deverell's patronising Earl of Clincham were absolutely in keeping with the spirit of the book.

At the close Daisy Ashford, accompanied by her adaptors, was prevailed upon to come on to the stage at the repeated calls of the audience.

She was obviously overcome, and simply said, "I cannot speak, but I thank you all very much."

Pictures on Back Page.

end *The Jealous Governes* by Angie. But this book, coming so soon after *The Young Visiters*, did not have the hoped-for success.*

The success of *The Young Visiters* continued through the twenties and the play was revived for one performance in 1928, with a cast composed of the children of actors, and little Margie was brought up to London to play the part of a guest in the Buckingham Palace scene.

Daisy and James bought a farm at Framingham Pigot, near Norwich, where James started a cut-flower business, and this flourished for some years. Unfortunately Daisy had inherited Emma's carefree way with money and neither she nor James were in the least businesslike. The large sums that accrued to her from her book quickly vanished, and the farm, in spite of James's undoubted flair for growing things, gradually sank into decay. Daisy's generosity, which had been overflowing in her prosperous years, was also a factor in their reduced circumstances. By the mid-thirties the farm had to be sold and, after a brief experiment in running a village inn, they moved to a house on the outskirts of Norwich where they lived until 1956.

Fortune, in the form of financial success, certainly failed to smile on any of the sisters, but the letters that flowed between them contained few complaints and their humour was undimmed by adversity. At their rare meetings talk and laughter went on far into the night and sometimes until the sun rose.

The Young Visiters brought in a small income and Daisy was occasionally asked to write an article or review children's books. During the war she began to write her autobiography, which she posted off, chapter by chapter, to Vera who copied it out on her elderly typewriter, laughing every now and then at Daisy's turn of phrase. Years later Margie

---

* Nevertheless all the stories have since been republished and are now available as follows: 'A Short Story of Love and Marriage', 'The True History of Leslie Woodcock' and 'The Jealous Governes' in *Love and Marriage*, illustrated by Ralph Steadman and introduced by Humphrey Carpenter (Oxford University Press, 1982); and 'Where Love Lies Deepest' and 'The Hangman's Daughter', with the hitherto unpublished 'The Life of Father McSwiney', in *The Hangman's Daughter and Other Stories*, introduced by Daisy Ashford's daughter, Margaret Steel (Oxford University Press, 1983).

Daisy in 1949

discovered her mother burning the entire typescript during a bout of spring cleaning.

In the war both Vera and Angie lost sons on active service while Daisy's family remained intact. Then, in the course of just over a year, she suffered three blows from which she never really recovered. In 1955 her elder son died, the following year James, and only two months later her beloved sister Vera. All three deaths were quite sudden.

Daisy, unable to look after herself, went to live with Margie and her growing family, who lived nearby, and who increasingly dealt with the reporters and interviewers from the press, radio and television; for as she grew older there was a revival of interest in *The Young Visiters* and her other stories. The fact that her entire output was produced in the last two decades of the nineteenth century made her something of a curiosity in the postwar world. Praise always took her by surprise and her frequent forgetfulness and her genuine modesty made her a difficult person to interview.

In November 1968, a musical version of her book was produced in London and Daisy was taken up to the first night, when she was introduced from the stage by Alfred Marks who played Mr Salteena. She was helped to her feet to acknowledge the applause of the audience, bewildered by the glare and the attention, and relieved when the spotlight moved away from her.

In the same year Angie died and Daisy slipped further into that shadowy world of the very old, her daughter often suffering the pain of being addressed by the names of people long dead. Although she appeared very frail, she moved about the house without much difficulty, but she preferred to sit by the fire smoking, a pastime that Emma used to condemn in both her and Vera, predicting an early death if it were persisted in. But despite her mother's foreboding Daisy lived to be ninety, the last of her lively generation, and having produced, all unwitting, a classic. She died on 15th January 1972.

Daisy in 1961, photographed by Robert Smithies for the *Guardian*